Titles in the *Super Profile* series

BSA Bantam (F333)
MV Agusta America (F334)
Norton Commando (F335)

Austin-Healey 'Frogeye' Sprite (F343)
Ferrari 250GTO (F308)
Ford GT40 (F332)
Jaguar D-Type & XKSS (F371)
Jaguar Mk 2 Saloons (F307)
Lotus Elan (F330)
MGB (F305)
Morris Minor & 1000 (ohv) (F331)
Porsche 911 Carrera (F311)

Further titles in this series will be published at
regular intervals. For information on new titles
please contact your bookseller or write to the
publisher.

ISBN 0 85429 335 3

A FOULIS Motorcycling Book

First published 1983

© **Haynes Publishing Group**

Published by:
Haynes Publishing Group
Sparkford, Yeovil,
Somerset BA22 7JJ

Distributed in USA by:
Haynes Publications Inc.
861 Lawrence Drive, Newbury
Park, California 91320, USA

Editor: Rod Grainger
Dust jacket design: Rowland Smith
Page Layout: Barry Griffiths
Colour photography: Andrew Morland
Road tests: Courtesy of
Peter Scatchard, *Motorcycle Sport*
and *Motor Cycle* (IPC)
Printed in England by: J.H.Haynes &
Co. Ltd

FOREWORD

Being renowned for my love of British motorcycles, it has given me particular pleasure to be able to write this first complete book about the Norton Commando. Although circumstances have been such that I have never had the opportunity to own a Commando, I did have very high respect for the plunger-sprung Model 7 Dominator twin that I purchased and ran during the early fifties. It proved to be outstandingly reliable and exceptionally fast for a machine of its day. Indeed, the only grounds on which I could have faulted it were its inability to improve on an all-round petrol consumption of 55mpg (though I rode it hard), and the nightmare of having to remove and replace the cylinder head, during decarbonising, due to those wretched nuts that had to be inserted upwards through the cylinder fins at the rear of the head. Even with the slimmest of box spanners it seemed one could only apply about $\frac{1}{32}$ of a turn at a time! Yet it seems incredible to me that what started out as the 500cc Dominator engine survived, albeit with continual modifications to the basic design, for almost three decades. Even Bert Hopwood could not have expected this splendid design to have survived for so long.

Many have helped me in putting this book together and first and foremost I would like to thank Mike Jackson of Andover Norton for not only supplying many of the historical photographs but also for checking the manuscript to a tight deadline over the Christmas holiday period. John Hudson read through the manuscript too, and I am equally indebted to him as a leading authority on the Norton marque. Chris Rogers and Pete Shoemark very kindly spent much time and effort in answering my questionnaire, to contribute the Commando owner's point of view. I would also like to thank a good friend in the local police force, whose name is best omitted for obvious reasons. His views about using the Interpol models on police duties added an extra and unusual area of interest to the owner's view section. In this context I am also indebted to Neale Shilton, for it was through the editing of his book *A Million Miles Ago* and from subsequent conversations that I learnt much about the origin and development of the Interpol models, for which he was responsible.

Chris Rogers and Mike Taverner very kindly made their machines available for many of the component part photographs, as did Guy Shoosmith of St. Mary Bourne, Hants. This latter gentleman has a very fine private collection of machines, the Mark 3 Electric Start model forming an integral part of this collection. The photographs showing the model differences and component parts were taken by Andrew Morland, who demonstrated yet again his professionalism with a camera. Other photographs were taken by Les Brazier of the Haynes Publishing Group or provided from the files of Andover Norton or *Motorcycle Sport.*

Phil Cox, Chairman of the Norton Owners Club, went to great lengths to ensure I was fully informed about all of the club's activities and even delivered material to me personally to make sure I met my deadline, thus becoming another person to whom I am greatly indebted. His spontaneous helpfulness suggested that membership of the club would be a most valuable benefit to those who own, or are contemplating the ownership of, a Commando.

Jeff Clew

HISTORY

Bert Hopwood laid the foundations of what was to be, much later, the Norton Commando twin. His early career in the motorcycle industry had commenced when he was employed by Ariel Motors to work for Val Page, the Chief Designer at the Selly Oak works during the late 1920s. He became acquainted with Edward Turner when the latter joined the company as a forward design engineer and when Turner left Ariel to work for Triumph, Hopwood went with him. Jack Sangster, the Chairman of Ariel Motors, had formed Ariel Motors (J.S.) Ltd when the original company had fallen on hard times, and later took over the complete motorcycle manufacturing activity of Triumph when it separated from the car manufacturing part of the business during 1935. Turner was appointed General Manager of the new Triumph motorcycle company and he invited Hopwood to join him as design assistant.

Hopwood worked closely with Turner when the latter evolved the Speed Twin model, the second and most successful of the Triumph vertical twin designs. He was well aware of the shortcomings of Turner's brainchild which, in the main, were a tendency for the cylinder head to overheat and for the engine itself to be a decided 'rattler' in terms of mechanical noise. When he left Triumph to join Norton Motors in April 1947 as Chief Designer, one of the attractions was the opportunity to design from scratch the twin-cylinder model that Norton so urgently needed at that time. The result was the Model 7, or Dominator twin as it was more popularly known, which was launched a week before the 1948 Earls Court Show. It was a vertical twin of 497cc capacity, having bore and stroke measurements of 66 x 72.6mm, and which featured plunger-type rear suspension similar to that employed by the ES2 single. But as he has since related in his book *Whatever Happened to the British Motorcycle Industry* (Foulis/Haynes), Hopwood did not have the free hand in the design that he would have liked.

The overheating of the Triumph engine had been caused by insufficient airflow, a problem that had been partly offset by the use of light alloy for the cylinder head and block when the competition models were developed. Norton production economies ruled out the use of alloy for these castings, so Hopwood got around the problem by splaying the exhaust ports outwards so that cool air was able to flow more freely over the cylinder head of the cast iron engine used in the new Norton twin. He would have liked a one-piece crankshaft assembly, but a combination of production problems and antiquated machine tools prevented this. As the best compromise he had to design a three-piece crankshaft that would have much greater strength than its Triumph counterpart and would incorporate detail differences to circumvent copyright infringement. The 'rattling' problem was avoided by using a single chain-driven camshaft. A new gearbox was designed to supersede the old, familiar upright type used on the single cylinder Norton models, and an entirely new frame with its associated cycle parts was created, although it proved necessary to fit the then current design of 'Roadholder' telescopic front forks. The overall appearance of the new model was enhanced by fitting a nicely styled petrol tank, recessed at the rear to accommodate the rider's knees. An oil pressure gauge was incorporated in the top panel, the panel itself having a fold line running down the middle.

Initially, the new vertical twin was for export only, as Britain was in need of all the money it could raise after the war. But by late 1949 the Dominator became available on the home market too, with the result that the road tests published in the two motorcycling weeklies began to have some meaning for the man in the street. Maximum speed under favourable conditions was not far from the magic 'ton', and about 2mph up on the maximum speed of the 500cc International model. Petrol consumption varied from 55 to 65mpg, depending on how the machine was ridden. In an emergency situation, both brakes would bring the machine to a halt in 30.5 feet from 30mph, good at the time. The overall weight of the machine was 438lb – not bad when one considers the weight of today's machines and that the engine was of cast iron.

Hopwood had intended to get an overhead camshaft version of the Dominator into production too, for he was aware of the need to reduce the overall width of the engine by locating centrally the valve drive gear – the machine could then be considered for racing. However, he had not reckoned on determined resistance from Joe Craig, who continued to pin his faith on the overhead camshaft singles from which he was still managing to extract extra power. It was internal politics that caused this overhead camshaft twin to be abandoned, Gilbert Smith, the Managing Director, maintaining that the standard twin would 'keep Norton safe' for the next decade or so. It mattered but little that

Hopwood would have needed only 18 months from the moment of its conception to get the proposed new Norton twin into production ....

The chance publication of a photograph in *Motor Cycling* on 26th July, 1951, showed a Dominator twin engine and gearbox mounted in one of the latest Norton 'featherbed' frames. It had been taken during the Dutch Grand Prix at Assen and, as the machine had a Birmingham registration, it seemed obvious that it was a prototype out on test. This was confirmed when, just before the 1951 Earls Court Show, Norton Motors announced a new de Luxe version of the standard Dominator Twin that utilised the 'featherbed' frame and was to all intents and purposes similar in appearance to the prototype. Finished in polychromatic grey and destined 'for export only', this new variant had swinging-arm rear suspension, shortened 'Roadholder' front forks and a new seat, mudguards, petrol and oil tanks. These changes in specification brought about a useful weight reduction of about 30lb. By now, Hopwood had moved on to BSA, having become thoroughly disillusioned by the working conditions and the internal politics he found it necessary to endure during his time at Bracebridge Street.

When Norton announced their 1953 programme during October 1952, all the spring frame models, including the standard Dominator twin, had been changed to incorporate swinging arm rear suspension. It was not a particularly tidy conversion; the front half of the frame appearing to follow the original layout, with the rear swinging-arm added almost as an afterthought. It was a heavy frame, too. In the case of the Model 7, the other most noticeable differences were the adoption of a flat dualseat and silencers that were of peardrop shape. The de Luxe 'featherbed' version was still for export only. Production continued along broadly similar lines for the 1954 and 1955 season models too, although by 1955 the de Luxe model, now catalogued as the Model 88, had become available on the home market with a welded-on subframe. However, times of major change were not far away.

During February 1953, Norton Motors had found itself in financial difficulties and a merger had been agreed with Associated Motor Cycles of Woolwich, this latter company acquiring the share capital of Norton. It was anticipated that the two companies would continue to retain their individual identities, as indeed proved the case. But soon the influence of the AMC Group could be detected when parts more closely associated with AJS and Matchless began to appear throughout the Norton range.

Bert Hopwood came back to Bracebridge Street during April 1956, initially in the capacity of an Executive Director. Despite earlier criticism of his Dominator twin engine by Joe Craig, Bert Hopwood was surprised to find it unchanged and still giving a good account of itself, confirming his suspicions that Joe Craig's unjustified criticism was because he did not welcome the intrusion the twin could have made into his world of the Norton singles. For the 1956 season, it was decided to drop the original Model 7 design, which had now been in production for eight years, leaving only the Model 88 twin, virtually unchanged, to represent the 500cc class. A newcomer, catalogued as the Model 99, added the option of a 596cc engine by increasing the bore and stroke of the 497cc engine to 68 x 82mm. In consequence, the Model 99 was no more than a Model 88 with a larger capacity engine, the frame and cycle parts being identical.

For the 1957 season, a third twin was added to the Norton range, mainly with sidecar use in mind, although it could also be ridden solo. Of 597cc capacity, it utilised the Model 99 engine, but differed in having a brazed lug cradle frame and a malleable iron engine cradle. With only a single front downtube, and having a multitude of lugs, it looked very untidy alongside the 'featherbed' type of frame and reflected AMC rather than Norton practice. Already, front and rear mudguards of AMC design had begun to make their appearance on models in the Norton range, and for the 1957 season a new gearbox, of AMC origin, replaced the original Norton design which Hopwood himself had updated when he designed the Model 7 Dominator. Other modifications for 1957 included a new front wheel hub and the fitting of separate chome-plated pressings to the sides of the petrol tank, to which the knee pads were affixed. The headlamp now had the switch, ammeter and speedometer fitted directly into the shell and there was also a redesigned rear chainguard as well as new silencers, tapered and streamlined in shape. One additional feature that applied only to the new Model 77 was a new design of oil tank, which was long and thin, and mounted on the right-hand side of the machine.

In many respects, the Model 77 represented a step backward rather than forward, even if the object of the exercise was to permit the attachment of a sidecar. Yet sidecars were no longer enjoying the popularity that at one time had made them an acceptable compromise for the man who wished to have family transport with the low running costs of a motorcycle. The advent of the cheap, second-hand saloon car had begun to make its impact, a trend that would soon establish itself more firmly and eventually render the sidecar outfit more or less obsolete. Not unexpectedly, the anticipated level of sales was never reached and by August 1958, the Model 77 was discontinued.

As far as 1958 was concerned, by far the most remarkable achievement was the entry of the former Sidecar World Champion, Eric Oliver, in the Isle of

Man Sidecar TT race. With no pretensions to winning, he set himself the challenge of obtaining a Replica by entering a Norton Dominator twin to which was attached a standard Watsonian Monaco sidecar, complete with lady passenger! At first, the Norton works thought he had taken leave of his senses and said openly that the outfit would not last a lap, but merely humiliate both driver and manufacturer. But they had not reckoned with Eric's unshakeable confidence in his own ability and his sheer persistence. With his passenger unable to do much in the way of leaning out to keep the weight down, Eric showed his mettle during practice, when he flung the outfit into corner after corner in his inimitable style. The sceptics began to modify their views and when it came to the race itself, Eric achieved the impossible. With a maximum speed that was at least 40mph down on the works BMWs, he completed 9 laps of the Clypse circuit to finish in 10th place at an average speed of 59.95mph and gained a Bronze Replica.

Albeit more placidly than usual, his passenger Pat Wise had played her part too. Until then, she had been more at home racing solo Velocettes, as a private entrant.

Apart from the decision to drop the Model 77 for the 1959 season, the Model 88 and 99 twins continued in production much as before, an AC alternator driven from the end of the crankshaft and coil ignition having replaced the DC dynamo and magneto that formed part of the original specification, in 1958. De Luxe versions of both twins were announced during November 1958, the difference being the use of a modified camshaft that provided improved performance. Strangely, this designation was short lived, for when further changes in specification were announced during August 1959, both models had their name changed to Dominator Standard. The modifications comprised the use of

the new 'slimline' featherbed frame which was narrower in profile and had a deeper $3\frac{1}{2}$ gallon petrol tank fitted. Performance was increased by modifying the valve lift and using larger diameter inlet valves, which in turn necessitated a new cylinder head with increased finning. Cosmetically, a new design of rear mudguard was fitted, and a new dualseat. Silencers of the absorption type were also specified. For those who required better weather protection, de Luxe versions of the 88 and 89 Models were reintroduced, in this instance having their rear ends enclosed by means of two quickly detachable panels similar to those fitted to the 250cc Jubilee twin. Earlier in the year it had been possible to obtain a chaincase, to fully enclose the final drive chain, as an optional extra.

Attempts were made to use up stocks of the spring frame used for the unsuccessful Model 77 in two ways. A modified version of this machine was made with the US export market in mind, having raised handlebars, shortened mudguards and a two-into-one exhaust system arranged on the right-hand side, for desert racing. The other version appeared at the 1958 Earls Court Show, finished in blue enamel and listed as the 'Nomad'. Here again, the model was earmarked for the export market but in this instance it was intended for normal road use.

During 1958, Gilbert Smith had retired from Norton Motors, handing over his position as Managing Director to Bert Hopwood. He had served the company well for 42 years and it was unfortunate that his service contract had not been renewed when he had only a few more years left before he reached the usual age of retirement. Hopwood tried in vain to have Gilbert Smith retained by appealing to the AMC Board and was saddened when Gilbert died shortly after he had left Bracebridge Street, at the age of 62.

Not much happened to the

Norton range by way of changes in specification until March 1961, when Sports Special versions of the 88 and 99 twins were introduced, mainly with clubman racing events in mind. The essential difference between these and the models continuing in production lay in the use of twin carburetters with polished ports, a high performance camshaft and the option of a two-into-one exhaust system. Yet hardly had these new models been announced, when Hopwood made his final break from Norton, having found AMC control of the company too repressive. He rejoined Triumph and was successful in recruiting Doug Hele soon afterwards, as Development Engineer. Doug had already contributed much to the development of the Norton twins, as was so clearly demonstrated during the 1961 Senior TT in the Isle of Man, so he too was sorely missed at Norton.

By now, the racing successes of the single cylinder Manx Nortons were on the decline. Joe Craig had left Bracebridge Street during 1955, to live in Holland, and was unfortunate enough to lose his life in Austria less than two years later as the result of a heart attack whilst driving his car. His successors, including Doug Hele, had done their utmost to try to keep the singles competitive, but clearly they were no match for the foreign multi-cylinder designs that now had the upper hand. 1961 proved to be a good year for Norton as far as the Senior TT was concerned, but it was not the first and second places by Mike Hailwood and Bob McIntyre that took all the limelight, or the first place in the Junior Race by Phil Read – the last ever Norton 'double'. Rather, it was a new machine which took third place in the Senior in the hands of Tom Phillis – the so-called 'Domiracer', a prototype based on the standard Dominator 88. The project had been kept secret for something like four years, this being the amount of time Doug Hele had required for development. As may be expected, the Domiracer differed in several respects from the Model 88, mainly in respect of a lighter and more compact 'featherbed' frame and the use of a five-speed gearbox. Remarkably, Phillis had very little first-hand experience of this machine, being limited to only a few practice laps during the week that preceded the race. Yet he recorded a shattering average speed of 100.36mph on his second lap and would undoubtedly have improved on his finishing position had he not found it necessary to ease off when he found the rear tyre was rubbing the swinging-arm fork. He also suffered some loss of performance when the tappet adjusters worked loose and slackened off. Later, some tests at MIRA showed his rev counter had been reading low, and could have been as much as 1000rpm on the optimistic side! When all of these factors are taken into account, it speaks volumes for Hele's expertise and makes one wonder what Hopwood's ohc version of the twin would have achieved had it not been vetoed by Joe Craig.

For the 1962 season, the capacity of the twin-cylinder engine was enlarged yet again, this time to 647cc by using bore and stroke measurements of 68 x 89mm. In consequence the 600cc Model 99 was dropped. Three versions of the new 650 were available, the Dominator 650 Standard, the Dominator 650 de Luxe, and the Dominator 650 Sports Special. The Standard model had a similar specification to that of the Model 99, apart from the larger capacity engine which had a higher compression ratio and a new design of cylinder head, a heavy duty clutch, and a wider section rear tyre. The de Luxe model was identical in specification but had the option of a rear end enclosure like that of the de Luxe versions of the 88 and 99 models. The 650 Sports Special, however, represented the determination of the company to retain their hold on the 'performance machine' sector

of the market. Earlier in the year, high performance versions of the 88 and 99 twins had been added to the range, representing 'spin off' from the development of the Domiracer. The new 650 Sports Special followed suit, but was unique in having a magneto for ignition whilst retaining the standard alternator, rectifier and battery for lighting and the associated electrical functions. All the SS models had a new light alloy cylinder head with parallel cast-in induction tracts, to permit the use of twin carburetters. Needless to say, quite a few of the 650SS models were entered for some of the long distance endurance races, like that held annually at Thruxton. They gave a good account of themselves too.

The underlying reason for introducing the 650cc models came as the result of Norton Motors opening up their own distributorship in the USA as the result of negotiations with Joe Berliner. Until then, their machines had been imported only in very small numbers. America needed a 650 Norton twin, and it was through the Berliner Corporation that the new models reached the shores of the USA. The initial negotiations had been made when Bert Hopwood was still with Norton Motors, an Americanised version of the 600 twins setting the ball rolling. This had been given the name Manxman and featured the raised handlebars that were a characteristic requirement of the US market. But it was a 650 twin that US riders really required, hence the 'stretched' 600cc engine.

The first signs of financial unrest within the AMC Group came during 1962, when it was announced that Bracebridge Street was to close and that, in the interest of rationalisation, the manufacture of Norton motorcycles would be transferred to Woolwich, where the marque would be amalgamated with Matchless. Needless to say, this was news that shook the motorcycling world, for

of all the British motorcycle manufacturers, Norton had a name and reputation that made it the cornerstone of the industry. The move took place during 1963, and coincided with the deletion of some models from the Norton range, including the 99 twins.

Before the move took place, there had been time to bring out yet another twin, which was to prove the last of the line to emerge from the Birmingham factory. This was the 73 x 89mm Atlas, which initially was earmarked for export only. In general specification it resembled the Dominator 650 Sports Special, the larger bore engine having a compression ratio of 7.6:1 and twin $1\frac{1}{8}$in diameter carburetters. An immensely powerful machine, it suffered the drawback that Turner and Hopwood experienced when they increased the capacity of the Triumph twin – that of vibration. The Atlas was a real shaker, and it was this aspect of the machine's character that influenced thought about the future of the design.

To follow the progress of the Norton twins after the move to Woolwich and the amalgamation with Matchless becomes increasingly difficult. There was such a high degree of interchange of parts that it became difficult to know what name should go on the tank of a machine that comprised a Norton engine in a Matchless frame, or vice-versa! The confusion did not last for long: in August 1966, the AMC Group found itself in such serious financial difficulties that a receiver had to be called in by the bank. Just a month later, terms had been agreed for the takeover by Manganese Bronze Holdings, of which Dennis Poore was Chairman. Stocks of the old machines were cleared during the next couple of years or so, whilst a new and much more exciting project got under way. Norton was saved, but Matchless went under, along with James and Francis Barnett who also formed part of the old AMC Group.

The Norton Atlas had undeniable potential as a high performance machine if only something could be done to alleviate the vibration problem which always becomes more acute in a vertical twin engine as the capacity is increased. It was left to two motorcycle development engineers to come up with the answer – Bernard Hooper and Bob Trigg, who were working under the control of Dr. Stefan Bauer, formerly associated with Rolls-Royce. Dr. Bauer had joined the new company – Norton Villiers Ltd – on 1st January 1967, to head a team who were to work on a design project that would lead to the manufacture of an entirely new Norton motorcycle. Using the Atlas engine as the basis for their investigation they came up with the novel idea of isolating the engine, gearbox and bearing of the swinging rear fork from the main frame by means of rubber bushes, so that the rider would no longer suffer from the effects of vibration transmitted through the frame. And so the famous 'Isolastic' suspension system was born, which was subsequently patented and earned for its inventors a prestigious award from Castrol for their meritorious contribution to motorcycling. The Norton Commando had come into being almost 20 years after Norton's first vertical twin had appeared on the market ....

The main features of the new machine, apart from the method of mounting the engine, gearbox and swinging arm pivot, were an engine with cylinders that sloped forward and a main frame with a massive $2\frac{1}{4}$ inch diameter top tube that supported a conventional duplex tube cradle to carry the engine, gearbox and swinging arm pivot sub-assembly. The engine was attached by means of rubber mountings to two small lugs on the front downtubes, and was bolted to engine plates at the rear through which the gearbox passed and to which it was anchored. These plates also carried the pivot bearing for the swinging arm fork and had two more attachment points, by means of rubber bushes, at the rear of the main frame. It was the function of the large diameter top frame tube to resist any torsional movement that would otherwise have necessitated more robust sub-assembly mountings. Viewed in retrospect, this answer to an age-old problem appears to be quite simple, especially when it is recalled that over the years motorcycle manufacturers have used rubber mountings in a variety of different forms to damp out vibration. However, they usually applied this approach to isolated components, rather than to complete assemblies. The Hooper and Trigg approach was the logical extension of these ideas with the advantage of keeping development costs well within the tight budget.

The Commando made its public debut at the 1967 Earls Court Show, in what was termed 'Fastback' form. Finished in silver (even a silver-painted engine), the only relief came from a bright orange-coloured seat which had 'ears' that projected forward on each side to blend in with the rear portion of the petrol tank. This latter component, like the base of the seat, was moulded in fibreglass, as was the tailpiece of the seat. Breaking away from old established practice, the petrol tank had no transfer affixed or any means of being able to identify the manufacturer of the machine. Instead, there was a green 'blob' in the position normally occupied by a transfer, which the company's advertising agents had determined would be part of the new corporate image. It proved to be a short-lived innovation when the machines went into volume production, but it lived on in the company's letterheads.

The production models came on to the market during February 1968, but with a more conservative finish. The frame was finished in black and the seat covered with a black material. The petrol tank was now finished completely in green, as was the tail end of the seat, whilst the engine retained its natural colours. After the initial launch, the Commando was to undergo many changes in specification, as detailed in the 'Evolution' section, until production finally ceased during October 1977. Perhaps the late Gilbert Smith had been right after all, for the twin had 'seen Norton safe' for just under three decades – three times as long as he had envisaged!

From a racing viewpoint the Commando had made its mark too, helped by sponsorship from John Player. Paul Dunstall had shown the potential of the latter day twins based on the Domiracer by purchasing most of the special parts that had been used in the development of the works' twins when the Norton Racing Shop closed down in 1962. The introduction of the 750 twin spurred him on and that year his machines took three World Records, as well as a 1st in the 1968 Isle of Man Production TT. His spine frame racers, ridden by Ray Pickrell, contributed to the 30 impressive racing successes gained by Dunstall Nortons during the period 1967-70.

The racing potential of the Commando had not escaped the attention of Dennis Poore, and in 1972 he offered road racer Frank Perris the opportunity of team managing Norton's bid for racing success. Frank was successful in obtaining the services of three extremely promising riders – Peter Williams, Dave Croxford and Mick Grant – each of whom had a string of racing successes behind them. Based at Thruxton aerodrome, not far from the factory at Andover to which Norton Villiers had moved after the take-over, they did their best to offer serious challenge to the opposition. They had their moments of glory, such as Williams' second place in the 750cc Production TT, but even with 'guest' riders of the calibre of Phil

Read, John Cooper and Tony Jefferies, they had little to show at the end of the year. 1973 was a little better, when Williams won the Formula 750 race during TT week, with Mick Grant 2nd. Unbelievably, Williams had completed the standing start lap at 106.58mph and his second lap at 107.27mph. But this was still not enough, and major success continued to elude them.

By this time, Formula 750 racing had come into prominence and two different versions of the 750cc Commando were being made in limited numbers, with racing specifically in mind. These were spin-offs from the early works-entered machines ridden by Phil Read, Peter Williams and others, one being an out-and-out 750 racer and the other a 750 production racer; the latter machine having the full lighting and other equipment necessary to meet the 750 cc Production Racing Class regulations. Both machines were homologated under the F.I.M. Regulations appertaining to the class under which they were to be entered, and their close allegiance to the original Commando was obvious. Production ceased when, in their wisdom, the FIM decided to abandon Formula 750 racing.

A spaceframe was designed for the 1974 season works racers, to house a Cosworth-designed, twin-cylinder engine to replace the now-ageing Atlas motor. As is so often the case, delivery of the new engine was delayed, so the old engine was installed in the new frame. Well down on speed, Williams and Croxford amazed everybody by finishing 1st and 4th in the Hutchinson 100, which gave reason for renewed hope. But it was not to be. Soon afterwards, Williams was seriously injured at Oulton Park and his racing career brought to a premature end. Croxford did his best to hold ends up, without success. So, when John Player withdrew their sponsorship at the end of the season, the end of Norton's bid for racing successes was clearly in sight. In only a comparatively short time, manufacture of the production models would cease too. The Norton twin, originally conceived by Bert Hopwood and Jack Moore in 1947 had been finally laid to rest.

EVOLUTION

When the Norton Commando was launched at the 1967 Earls Court Show, it was catalogued officially as the Model 20 Mark III. Production commenced in earnest during February 1968, the specification being that which was later classified as the Fastback. Although the colour changes already mentioned in the 'History' section relate to the early production models, the name Fastback was not used officially until March 1969. By then the frame had been stiffened by an extra tube running from the steering head to the rear end of the spine. User experience dictated the use of a raised and narrower centre stand to prevent 'grounding' problems, whilst the opportunity was taken to use the traditional Norton transfer on the sides of the petrol tank.

At the same time the Commando 'S' was introduced. This was similar in specification to the Fastback, without gaiters, and a 2½ gallon petrol tank. Not so obvious was the use of softer rubber engine mountings and stiffer rear suspension. September 1969 saw the positioning of the contact breaker on the Fastback models at the front of the timing cover, within a compartment covered by an inspection cap retained by two screws. This dispensed with the horizontally-mounted distributor at the rear of the timing chest. It also necessitated taking the tachometer drive from the camshaft.

During March 1970, a third model was added to the range, the Commando Roadster. This resembled the 'S' model, but was fitted with low level exhaust pipes, the silencers of which were tilted upwards and of the reverse cone type. It had the catalogue designation '20 Mark III SS'. It seems as though the demand for the Commando 'S' model had not reached the level expected, for it was discontinued during June 1970.

The Commando Fastback was restyled during September 1970 by fitting an upswept exhaust system with reverse cone silencers. It was then catalogued as the 'Commando Fastback Mark II'. But this model too was short-lived, as it was discontinued only a matter of four months later. It was replaced by the Fastback Mark III, which had slimmer front forks without gaiters, alloy handlebar levers and electrical switches, modified centre and prop stands, a modified rear chainguard and a different oil tank and side panels. Another change was made, to the front wheel which now carried a tyre of 4.10 x 19 in. size. At the same time the Commando Roadster was deleted from the catalogue and replaced by a Mark II version of similar specification to the new Fastback Mark III. It differed only from the latter in having side panels in a colour that matched that of the petrol tank. Both the new models were listed officially as the '20M3S'.

American influence dictated the need for yet another model variant, the Commando SS, or 'street scrambler', which was announced in May 1971. Features of this model were a two gallon petrol tank, an upswept exhaust system, and a sprung mudguard fitted to the upper forks. It was followed a month later by the Fastback LR model, similar to the Fastback Mark III but fitted with a four gallon petrol tank and a restyled seat. Yet another variant appeared during May, the Commando Hi-Rider made especially for those who had an inclination towards the chopper cult; this latest model featured the obligatory raised handlebars, a two gallon petrol tank and chopper-style seat.

The Commando SS had a short life too, for it was dropped after being in production for only five months. But there were soon other models to take its place and add to the ever-growing number of Commando variants.

January 1972 heralded the arrival of the Fastback Mark IV, which differed from its Mark III predecessor in having a new crankcase with the breather at the end. More obvious was the fitting of a front wheel disc brake and for the first time, direction indicators. The Fastback LR followed suit and was redesignated the Fastback Mark IV. The Roadster Mark II also took on a similar specification to become the Mark IV, as did the Hi-Rider, although the latter continued to use a front wheel drum brake. These was also a new model, the Commando Interstate. Similar in specification to the Roadster Mark IV, it was fitted with the new high performance 'Combat' engine, identified by black-painted cylinder barrels, a five gallon petrol tank, a longer dualseat, flatter profile handlebars and differently shaped silencers that were mounted much lower.

There had been high hopes for the Combat engine, a high performance version of the standard unit capable of giving 65 bhp at 6500 rpm – an increase of 5bhp. One of the modifications had involved increasing the compression ratio from 8.9:1 to 10:1 (Doug Hele having limited it to 7.3:1 in the Atlas engine), with only a minor modification to the main bearings. By the time several thousand of these engines have been made, warranty claims were flooding in, mainly as the result of premature main bearing failure. It was not an easy problem to resolve, especially as the compression ratio increase had been achieved by machining the joint face of the cylinder head. The inclusion of an aluminium alloy head gasket helped to put matters right by lowering the compression ratio, although this was only a temporary expedient. Sooner or later the head gasket started to leak, giving rise to further problems. The Combat engine gave the Commando a bad name at this time and it was some time before the whole unfortunate episode was lived down.

The Fastback Mark IV and the Fastback LR Mark IV were discontinued in January 1973. Just a couple of months later, the Roadster Mark IV received further attention, possibly as a result of main bearing problems that had now become manifest in the standard engines. Rumours abounded concerning the reasons, the most popular opinion being that the maximum cruising rpm quoted at 7000rpm, some 500rpm above maximum power development, caused excessive crankshaft flexing. True or not, the Fastback Mark V that superseded the Mark IV version had a lower compression ratio, modified main bearings and raised overall gearing – all moves to give the engine longer life. A Hi-Rider Mark V followed suit, whilst the Interstate, the model that had given rise to the engine problems described, had the new specification standard engine fitted in place of the now obsolete Combat unit. However, as subsequent events showed, these modifications were only temporary measures to use up the existing stock of 750cc engines. By October 1973 all the 750cc models were discontinued – the 850cc models that had supplemented them from April onwards had now superseded them.

The 850cc engine (or 828cc to be correct) came into being by increasing the bore size of the

750cc design to 77mm, the 89mm stroke being retained. Three models were announced initially, the 850 Roadster, the 850 Hi-Rider and the 850 Interstate, each with a specification identical to that of its 750cc Mark V counterpart. The new engine had an adequate reserve of power and suffered from none of the stresses that had caused the earlier bearing failures. Nonetheless, further development work permitted the introduction of the Mark 1A Roadster and Interstate models in September 1973. Both these models had raised overall gearing and more effective silencers, as well as a new design of plastic air cleaner box. Four months later, the older Mark 1 versions of the Roadster, Hi-Rider and Interstate were discontinued.

Little changed on the 850cc models already in production during 1974, apart from painting the cylinder barrels black, improving the cylinder head porting and fitting a dualseat with a quilted top.In consequence, the Hi-Rider model was redesignated the Mark 2, and the Roadster and Interstate models the Mark 2A. Bright spot of the year was the introduction of the John Player Replica in April. This machine was similar to the Roadster Mark 2A but had a race-type fairing, painted in the John Player colours, fitted with twin headlamps. Dropped handlebars and rear-set footrests, brake pedal and gearchange lever completed the racing image, even though the machine was very much a sheep in wolf's clothing. Clearly Norton had taken the opportunity to cash-in on the potential of the Peter Williams/Dave Croxford racing models that were enjoying considerable popularity at the race tracks whenever they appeared. Doubtless, these are the models that will acquire an appreciating 'collectors value' as time progresses, as they were made in comparatively small numbers.

By February 1975 the John Player Replica had been dropped, after only 10 months production,

along with the Roadster Mark IA and 2A models, the Interstate Mark 1A and 2A, and the Hi-Rider Mark 2. The ranks were beginning to thin down ....

By now, it was an acknowledged fact that virtually every Japanese motorcycle was equipped with an electric starter which, in some cases, had led to dispensing with the old, familiar kickstarter. It was no longer considered effeminate to start a machine by means other than a kickstarter, so Norton pandered to this change in outlook by bringing out the Mark 3 Commando during March 1975 in which an electric starter formed part of the specification. Fortunately, it was decided to retain the original kickstarter, which often as not was needed to start the engine. As anyone who has tried to start an 850cc Norton twin will know, it is not an easy task using the kickstarter, even when the correct technique is known. In consequence the electric starter had a hard time, the more so if the battery was a little down and the ambient temperature was low. Unless the pistons happened to be in exactly the right position, and the vaporisation of the petrol in the carburettors was good, it was more of an electrical 'assister' than a starter, which would soon drain the battery. But fitted it was, the other modifications comprising a rear disc brake operated by the right foot, a new control panel, foot gearchange on the left-hand side, and a hinged dualseat. The transposition of the gearchange and brake pedal controls had been brought about by the need to meet changes in legislation that had occurred within the USA, which was still a useful export outlet.

Just two models now continued in production, the Mark 3 Electric Start Interstate and Roadster. The specification remained unchanged for a further $2\frac{1}{2}$ years until October 1977, when production of the Commando models ended completely.

Although it can be said that the Commando never quite achieved the level of success that had been anticipated during its life span of almost 10 years, it had made its mark on motorcyclists all over the world. In the UK it won the *Motor Cycle News* 'Machine of the Year' competition for five successive years, from 1968 to 1972, and was widely accepted as the first 'Superbike'. In the USA it had acquitted itself exceptionally well in some of the early road tests conducted by *Cycle World* and others, whilst in a Drag Race Championship held at Atco, New Jersey, on November 1st, 1970, Tom Christenson had recorded 157.06mph at the end of the quarter mile with a twin-engined Norton and 139.10mph with a single-engined dragster. Many other similar achievements had helped to keep the Norton flag flying and when it was finally lowered, there were many that mourned the passing of such a great machine.

Significant changes by engine number

Reproduced from 'Commando Service Notes' by kind permission of the Norton Owners Club

126,125: First Commando, Feb '68. Silver tank, panels and frame — orange seat. Green blob on tank.

131,180: Now called 'Fastback'. Conventional colour scheme. Gusset below headstock replaced by horizontal bracing tube under tank (The first frames broke).

131,257: First 'S' type made for American market. Small rounded (Roadster type) tank. High level parallel pipes left hand side, with reverse cone shape silencers. Points on the end of the camshaft, rev. counter drive inboard. Six volt coils with ballast resistor. 1971.

133,668: Fastback receives 'S' type technical mods. Points, coils etc.

135,140: First 'Roadster' with low pipes, upswept silencers, reverse cone absorption type.

139,571: 'Fastback Mk II' fitted with Roadster exhaust system

142,534: 'Mk II Roadster,' 'Mk III Fastback', same 4:10 tyres on both wheels. Fork gaiters and F/bed type yokes dropped, bare chrome stanchions introduced. Lucas h/bar lever switches and indicators introduced. Centre stand mounted on g/box. Shock absorber fitted in rear wheel.

Jan '72: Consecutive engine numbers which had continued since W.W. II abandoned. New system and numbers introduced.

200,001: 'Fastback Mk IV', 'Roadster Mk IV'. New crankcase castings, with breather behind c/case (not from end of camshaft). First double roller main bearings.

200,976: First Combat engine. Compression ratio raised to 10:1 by machining head, double S camshaft fitted. Black barrels, 32mm carbs. Disc brake right-hand side behind fork leg. Models now 'Fastback' and 'Roadster'.

212,278: 'Interstate'. Larger black or blue (5 gal) tank, seat longer. Low level Interstate silencers. (Most Combat engines were later modified to standard engine specification and stronger main bearings fitted, i.e. Superblends (barrelled rollers). Small sump plug introduced, later models with car type oil filter. 16H type (pre-war) front brake shoes with speedo drive clearance no longer used in Commando rear wheel. (Shame!).

220,000: Combat engine abandoned but 32mm carbs

retained. Roadster Mk V, Interstate Mk V only. No more Fastbacks. Black instrument pods.

230,000: Square rear light. Different fork geometry. Box section head steady.

230,935: Last 750 Commando (unless you know better?)

300,001: April '73, first 850 Mk I. Barrel fixings altered, bronze clutch plates fitted, balance pipe in exhaust pipes. Strengthened swinging arm, larger sump plug reintroduced.

306,591: Mk IA. Larger, quiet airbox and annular discharge (bean can) silencers. Candy apple red tank also available. Chainguard plastic extension added. 2nd gear ratio raised by one tooth (to reduce noise readings).

307,091: Slimmer 'Interstate' tank, $4\frac{1}{2}$ gals approx.

307,311: 850 Mk IIA. Improved paint, 30mm ports but 32mm carbs (for flexibility). Various small detail mods., such as mud flaps, third sleeve gear bush added. Black and blue tanks dropped, red and a few "traditional" silver tanks. Fork gaiters reintroduced and lower bars. Tacho drive oil leak reduced (supposedly).

309,600: Larger, stronger kickstart.

SPECIFICATION

Commando 750 & 850

Model	Commando 750	Commando 850
Bore and stroke (mm)	73 x 89	77 x 89
Cubic capacity (cc)	745	828
Compression ratio	8.9:1	8.5:1
Bhp	58 @ 6800rpm	60 @ 5900rpm
Gear ratios:		
4th	4.84:1	4.2:1
3rd	5.9:1	5.1:1
2nd	8.25:1	6.8:1
1st	12.4:1	10.7:1
Sprocket sizes:		
Engine	26	26
Clutch	57	57
Final drive	19	22
Rear wheel	42	42
Suspension:		
Front	Teles	Teles
Rear	S/arm	S/arm
Tyre sizes:		
Front (in)	3.00 x 19*	4.10 x 19*
Rear (in)	3.50 x 19*	4.10 x 19*
Brake diameter:		
Front	8in tls drum	10.7in disc
Rear	7in drum	7in drum*
Chain size:		
Front	$\frac{3}{8}$ in triplex	$\frac{3}{8}$ in triplex
Rear	$\frac{5}{8}$ x $\frac{3}{8}$in	$\frac{5}{8}$ x $\frac{3}{8}$in
Fuel tank capacity	$3\frac{1}{4}$ galls*	$2\frac{1}{2}$ galls*
Oil tank capacity	5 Imp pint	5 Imp pint
Gearbox oil capacity	0.75 Imp pint	0.75 Imp pint
Generator:		
Type	Alternator	Alternator
Output (watts)	110	110

Battery capacity (amp/hr)	8	10*
Points gap (in)	0.015	0.015
Ignition timing (BTDC)	28°	28°
Wheelbase (in)	56¾	57
Ground clearance (in)	6	6
Seat height (in)	31	31
Overall width (in)	26	26
Dry weight (lb)	418	418-430*
Years of manufacture	1967-73	1973-77

*Notes

The specification details listed are differentiated only by the model's engine capacity and are therefore subject to variation in certain areas as the result of other differences in machine specification. For example, fuel tank capacity can vary from two gallons to five and a quarter gallons, depending on whether the model is of the Hi-Rider or Interstate category. In consequence, the overall weight of the machine will vary within certain limits too.

Machines fitted with the ill-fated 745cc Combat engine have a compression ratio increased to 10:1, which represents an increase in power output to 65bhp at 6500rpm. Made in limited numbers, the two racing models show an improvement even on these figures. Both models have an engine with the compression ratio raised to 10.25:1, which gives the 750 Racer a power output of 73bhp at 7000rpm and the 750 Production Racer 70bhp at 6500rpm. A number of options were available with either model specification, selected by the prospective owner at the time of placing the order.

The Electric Start models introduced during March 1975 featured a 10.7 inch rear disc brake in place of the 7 inch diameter rear drum brake fitted previously. A larger capacity battery became a necessity with the fitting of the solenoid-operated starter motor and as the result of these additions, the overall weight of these models increased to approximately 460lb.

Police machines of the Interpol type had a special high output generator to handle the additional electrical demand from the two-way radio, sirens and special lighting equipment.

ROAD TESTS

MOTOR CYCLE, 11 SEPTEMBER 1968

745cc NORTON COMMANDO

No new model introduced in the past decade has made such a big impact as the Norton Commando. It was first seen at the London Show last September and greeted with enthusiasm, though in some cases the welcome was reserved until production machines were available.

Motor Cycle road test

They were ready in May and experience on the road showed that the Norton marque had come back with a bang. The terrific power of the modified 745 cc Atlas twin was a new experience now it was rubber-mounted in an ingenious frame which did, in fact, virtually eliminate the effects of high-frequency vibration.

The sceptics retired to swallow their doubts. Overnight the Commando became the most-sought-after large-capacity roadster on the market.

Something more exhaustive than an orthodox road test was called for if the full potential of this bike was to be assessed. Thus TYT 63F was flown across the Channel in July after the routine performance figures had been obtained at the MIRA proving ground.

To say that the Commando showed up well would be grudging praise. In a 2,000-mile trip it proved a distance-devourer *par excellence*. Yet it was equally satisfying to ride in heavy traffic; on byroads in Italy and Switzerland, and high on alpine passes. It gave a new dimension to the sort of riding we have known on parallel twins in the past 20 years.

In short, the Commando provides an over-115 mph maximum speed, an acceleration graph like the side of a house, relatively light fuel consumption at high cruising speeds, woofling docility when required and a riding position that ensures complete comfort. All this, with a commendably low level of mechanical and exhaust noise.

At home

The basic Atlas engine is no newcomer. Its Commando application involved far more than installing it with a forward inclination in rubber mountings. Much development work has been completed. While it retains its capacity for producing beefy torque at low revolutions it is equally at home revving freely at

6,800 rpm and pushing out nearly 60 bhp.

In fact, with the standard 19-tooth gear-box sprocket fitted, the maximum speed of 117 mph obtained equals 7,200 rpm. The engine has ample margins and revs of this order are completely safe, but a 21-tooth sprocket is available if preferred. For high-speed riding it is, in practice, rarely necessary to exceed 5,000 rpm in any gear. The spread of power is so wide that, for example, a whiff

The comfortable riding position and taut feel of the Commando enable it to be ridden with satisfying verve on twisty roads

of throttle in top gear moves the speedometer needle very smartly from, say, 75 to 100 mph—invaluable when mile-eating on the fast, though far-from-straight, major roads in eastern France.

With such an ample supply of power, pass storming in the Alps was a really enjoyable exercise. Gradient and traffic baulks could be dealt with by the zippy yet unobtrusive acceleration.

Less orthodox

It was no hardship to use the indirect gears when necessary. The ratios are happily chosen and could be engaged rapidly and positively—from third to top as easily and quietly without clutch operation as with it.

The clutch is one of the Commando's less orthodox features. It has a diaphragm (with four friction plates) and is capable of dealing with more torque than the earlier, coil-spring clutch. It takes up the drive a shade more quickly but, apart from that, is better in every way. It proved light to operate, freed completely at all times and showed no signs of slipping or becoming overheated.

Handling is well up to the traditional Norton standards. The Commando has that taut, manageable feel at all speeds that encourages clean, stylish cornering. It keeps on line, can be flicked confidently through close-coupled S-bends and does not waver when banked over on bumpy surfaces.

The silencers limit banking angle but not to an unrealistic extent. Side and centre stands are well tucked away though they are slightly difficult to reach and push down with the foot.

Slight flutter

Steering is rock steady at all speeds above about 40 mph. Below that, there is slight handlebar flutter if the hands are re-

Inclined forward in the new frame, the 745 cc, twin-cylinder Atlas engine packs beefy power right through the range

moved from the grips. It is unnoticed in normal circumstances and might never be apparent unless the no-hands test is made.

The twin-leading-shoe front brake was, as expected, excellent, but the single-leading-shoe rear brake lacked power and occasionally failed to free properly. On the whole, braking was satisfactory (31 ft from 30 mph) but no more.

As mentioned earlier, the rider is well insulated from engine vibration. This factor alone is a comfort boost, especially on a 400-plus daily mileages such as undertaken during the text. But there is more to Commando comfort than this.

The riding position—the placing of the seat, handlebar grips, footrests and

controls—is spot on and the only possible criticism might be that the well-padded dualseat, at 31 in from ground level, is a bit high for some riders.

Starting was invariably easy—usually one prod on the pedal was enough. With the engine cold the only difference was to close the air lever. With next-to-no warming up, the engine would idle re-

The Commando has a completely new frame layout yet retains the powerful, thoroughbred lines long associated with high-performance Nortons

liably at only a shade over 600 rpm. Despite much hard riding, the twin Amal Concentric carburettors retained their slow-running settings and balance.

The electrical side, too, was faultless. During the continental trip it proved to be properly weatherproofed. The bike was usually parked in the open and on one occasion it was ridden for 10 hours in continuous rain. The engine never missed a beat.

Lighting permitted 80-mph cruising in the dark. A much-appreciated practical feature is the easily-operated toggle switch in the headlamp shell. Very useful, too, is the headlamp-flasher button in the dipswitch/horn console on the left side of the handlebar.

Another practical feature is the rear-chain oiler. It kept the chain lightly lubricated without surplus oil reaching the wall of the tyre. The chain needed adjustment at approximately 800-mile intervals.

Over the long continental mileage, some of it at high cruising speeds, the fuel consumption worked out at a shade over 50 mpg—lighter than usual with some machines of smaller capacity. Premium-type fuel, 98 octane, was used. The engine could be made to pink on this fuel but not seriously enough to warrant a higher-octane diet.

Oil consumption was 300 miles to the pint. This is thought to be higher than average but there was no obvious explanation. The exhaust was not smoky and the engine remained free from serious leaks.

Accessibility for servicing is good. A quickly detachable panel on the left below the seat nose reveals the battery.

Staffman Peter Fraser, who used the Commando for his visit to the ISDT venue at San Pellegrino in Italy, refuelling on his way back across France

745 cc NORTON COMMANDO

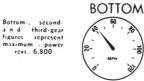

Bottom-, second- and third-gear figures represent maximum - power revs, 6,800.

ACCELERATION

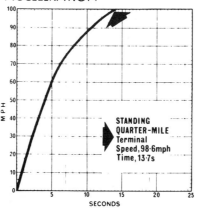

STANDING QUARTER-MILE
Terminal Speed, 98·6 mph
Time, 13·7 s

FUEL CONSUMPTION

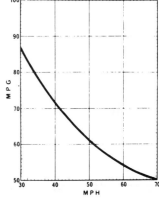

The seat itself can be removed in seconds without spanners. Tools are stored in a compartment in the glass-fibre tail fairing.

A single-bolt fixing for the cast-aluminium primary chain-case makes inspection and servicing unusually easy.

The Commando has set a new high in the field of big-capacity machines for which Britain has been famous for so long. It deserves the welcome it received when production started and the big reputation it is building now more and more machines are reaching world markets.

specification

ENGINE: Capacity and type. 745 cc (73 x 89mm) overhead-valve, parallel twin. Bearings: crankshaft supported in a roller bearing on the drive side and a ball bearing on the timing side; plain big ends and small ends. Lubrication: dry sump; oil-tank capacity, 5 pints. Compression ratio: 8.9 to 1. Carburettors: twin Amal Concentric, 30mm-diameter choke; air slides operated by handlebar lever. Impregnated-paper air-filter element. Claimed power output: 58 bhp at 6,800 rpm.
TRANSMISSION: Primary by ⅜in. triplex chain with movable gear box for adjustment; secondary by ⅝ x ⅜in chain. Clutch; multi-plate, with diaphram-spring. Gear ratios: 12.4, 8.25, 5.9, 4.84 to 1. Engine rpm at 30 mph in top gear: 1,850.
ELECTRICAL EQUIPMENT: Ignition by capacitor and twin coils. Charging by 110-watt alternator through rectifier and diode to 8-amp-hour battery. Headlamp: 7in-diameter, with 50/40-watt main bulb.
FUEL CAPACITY: 3¼ gallons.
BRAKES: 8in-diameter, twin-leading-shoe front; 7in-diameter rear
TYRES: Avon ribbed front, 3.00 x 19in; Avon GP rear, 3.50 x 19in.
SUSPENSION: Norton Roadholder telescopic fork with two-way hydraulic damping; pivoted rear fork controlled by Girling spring-and-hydraulic units with three-position adjustment for load.
DIMENSIONS: Wheelbase, 56¾in; ground clearance, 6in; seat height, 31in; all unladen.
WEIGHT: 418 lb, including half a gallon of fuel and full oil tank.
PRICE: £456 19s 4d, including British purchase tax.
ROAD TAX: £10 a year; £3 13s for four months.
MANUFACTURERS: Norton Villiers Ltd, Norton Matchless Division, 44 Plumstead Road, London, SE18.

performance

(Obtained by "Motor Cycle" staff at the Motor Industry Research Association's proving ground, Lindley, Leicestershire.)

MEAN MAXIMUM SPEED: 116 mph (14¼-stone rider wearing two-piece trials suit)
HIGHEST ONE-WAY SPEED: 117 mph (still air)
BRAKING: From 30 mph to rest on dry tarmac, 32ft.
TURNING CIRCLE: 13ft 9in.
MINIMUM NON-SNATCH SPEED: 18 mph in top gear.
WEIGHT PER CC: 0.56 lb.

NORTON COMMANDO

BY PETE SCATCHARD

NORTON'S lone runner in the roadster motorcycle stakes has been with the buying public for some seven years now.

The Commando 750 having now been replaced by the 850, readers may question the value of a long-term assessment of the former. However, the two machines do share the bulk of components, so we felt that many of the remarks appertaining to the little 'un could be read across to big brother, and such a report could thus prove of value to those contemplating the purchase of a new machine as well as those scouring through the second-hand market.

Heart of the machine is a pushrod OHV vertical twin engine, unfashionably over square, driving an equally unfashionable four-speed box via a triplex primary chain and dry multi-plate diaphragm spring clutch. The engine / transmission package is mounted in a spine type frame via the patented Isolastic rubbers, permitting movement in the vertical plane, thus absorbing engine vibration, wide thrust faces allied with close (10 thou) clearances in the mounts preventing movement in the horizontal plane that could otherwise make for interesting handling. A stripped down version of the long established Roadholder fork clutches a Norton-Lockheed disc braked front wheel, while the rear end is suspended by a pair of Girling shocks. Onto this basic machine is bolted a variety of tanks, seats, exhaust systems, side covers, handlebars and headlamps to form the current range of Roadster, Interstate, Hi-Rider and JP Replica versions, although Fastback, LR, S Type and SS variants have also been produced.

Despite the antiquated design, based on Bert Hopwood's 1947 Model 7, there's no shortage of effort from the big motor, whatever its detail form. The standard

750 mill runs on an 8.9 to 1 cr, a thicker solid copper or aluminium head gasket offering reductions down to below 8 to 1. The Combat motor uses the same pistons and a remachined head to achieve a cr of 10.2 to 1, breathing through two 32mm Amal Concentrics in place of the standard 30mm affairs. Perhaps the most unusual feature of the Norton Heavyweight twin motor is the integral head and rocker box, the rockers being located in the main head casting through the tappet inspection covers on press fit spindles sealed by small cover plates. Exhaust pipes are located in the head by large finned gland nuts, screwing directly into the casting. These form probably the biggest single source of irritation in the engine design, since despite the adoption of solid iron gaskets and a tab washer to lock gland nut to head, the exhaust pipes can be found jangling merrily away every 1,000 miles or so, whereupon a special spanner of monstrous proportions is required, plus a modicum of care to avoid overtightening and stripping of the threads. Solid skirt pistons featuring two compression rings, the top one chromed, and a Triflex oil control ring run in a bore machined directly from the cast-iron block.

Bore wear is minimal, the large paper element air filter effectively preventing the normal air-borne abrasive particles from doing their usual worst. Stellite tipped valves run in cast-iron guides, the inlets fitted with oil seal caps to overcome oil burning problems experienced at one time, large diameter aluminium push rods transmitting the cam lift via cam followers running in bores machined in the front of the block. The camshaft, buried in the front of the crankcases, runs in phosphor-bronze bushes, driven by a short chain. This requires checking for tension every

25,000 miles on

10,000 miles or so, and replacing about every 30,000 — no large expense or great effort is required, but it's another niggle regarding the engine design, and by the time twin sprockets, a chain and the necessary slipper adjuster had been fitted it would surely have been cheaper from a production angle to utilise gear pinions to transmit rotation from crankshaft to camshaft.

If chains are to be used, an external and preferably automatic tensioner should be incorporated, as per Honda OHC drive systems, as the present set up requires the contact breaker unit to be removed, and thus the engine retimed every time the tension's checked! The valve actuating mechanism is virtually bulletproof, although there are the occasional tales of stellite tips coming adrift from the followers, accompanied by interesting noises!

Major source of Commando engine problems has been the crank assembly, a forged steel bolted up crankshaft running in roller bearings. Being but a two-bearing affair, crankwhip occurs at high revs, causing the edges of the rollers to take more than their fair share of the load, breaking up the hardened tracks. The problem's been eliminated by the adoption of Fagg "Superblend" bearings, the rollers featuring a slight taper, thus eliminating the line contact. Con-rods are forged aluminium with steel big-end caps, the big ends being white metal backed plain bearings. Gudgeon pins run direct in the small-end eye, this and the big-end assembly being accepted as almost 100 per cent reliable.

End result of all this is a motor producing a claimed 60 bhp (SAE) at 6,500 rpm, redlined at 7,000, with peak torque at approx 5,000. These figures, allied to a dry weight of 415 lbs should mean some very adequate performance, and sure enough it

goes! Quick rather than stunningly fast, there's a regular indicated 110 mph available, with the bonus of approaching 120 with everything set as per book, and some mucho rapido acceleration up to 90 or so, at which point things start to quieten down. Norton claim a 0-60 time of just under five seconds, but as with most such figures it's a trifle academic — you need a nice Shell Grip surface, a quarter mile of straight, clear road and a healthy lack of mechanical sympathy to achieve such figures. Suffice to say that there's little, if anything, that'll stay with you out of the box, initial acceleration being rather quicker than a Honda 750's, but tailing off a little earlier than the Four.

The outstanding engine characteristic is the tremendous torque that the tall motor produces. It'll pull from a mere 1,000 rpm, while at two grand the throttle can be opened back to the stop without inducing a trace of fluffing, pulling smoothly until at about 3,500 the engine note changes and the mill really starts to soar away. Such willingness to pull from low revs proves a real boon in heavy traffic, and is ideal for winding through mountain roads, when the machine can be left in third gear all day, providing a 15-90 mph speed range.

It is therefore unfortunate that, while isolating the rider from the ever-present vibration at higher revs, the Isolastic mount's limited flexibility allows the large amplitude, low frequency vibration at low revs to be transmitted to the cycle parts. To be fair, this is hardly felt as vibration, more as a low down rumbling judder, and that's not apparent on small throttle openings below 2,000 rpm. The judder's at its worst when accelerating from low revs up to 3,500, when the mirrors are really a-tingle, then all of a sudden, the rhythm of the engine

matches the resonance of the Isolastic units and, just like flicking a switch, the "bad vibes" are but a memory, remaining so from there on up.

Above 3½ grand, the mounts really do their work, and the rider's totally isolated from the still vibrating engine, although still, of course, subject to shocks and judders from the suspension, this being more noticeable than usual due to the absence of other rider stimulii! The price to be paid is in the maintenance of the Isolastics, as the gap twixt spacer and mounting requires frequent checking and adjustment by shimming if the normal standard of handling is to be expected. Not a difficult job, the manufacturer recommends checking at 10,000 mile intervals, but this is little short of ludicrous — a 2,000 mile interval is about the maximum one can manage before excessive sideplay becomes apparent and a few more, very cheap shims are required. This kind of constant need for maintenance is one of the things one seems to have to accept on British bikes, though it would seem technically quite feasible to design either a no wear or self adjusting system.

Long regarded as the mass production experts on handling, and with good reason with such stalwarts as the Garden Gate and Featherbed frames under their belt, Norton dropped the long established full duplex frame in order to introduce the rubber mounted Commando, a complete re-design being essential to enable the swinging arm to be joined rigidly to the engine/gearbox unit, thus preserving the fixed relationship between the transmission components, yet permitting this "powerhouse" package to be flexibly mounted in the frame via the Isolastic bushing. Not unnaturally, the first question asked was not the usual "Wot'll it do?" — after all, the

engine was basically Atlas, but "Wot's it 'andle like?"

Comparisons were invariably made with the Featherbed, mostly uncomplimentary, but after a while many previously Featherbed owning riders started to revise their opinions. To judge, it's perhaps wiser and fairer to do so by performance, rather than by comparison. In its day, the Featherbed ruled supreme, together, in my opinion, with the Velo, marked by a very heavy front end, giving rock like stability on bumpy bends; today, the Commando must come right at the top of the heavyweight's handling tree, although its characteristics in this department are totally different.

A light front end produces a slight waggling of the bars at low speed, noticeable when riding one handed, and a delicate feel at high speed — a new approach is required, a sensitive one, reliant more on backside and foot than arm steering, but once one's learnt the technique and one's initial anxiety at this rather nervous feel to the steering reassured, it's predictable and very, very good. Ground clearance is positively massive, although large bumps when heavily laden and laid down round steep left handers produces interesting noises from the centre stand's roll-on extension.

Bumpy bends tend to cause the machine to wander a little, while heavily loaded it's possible to be nearly flung off hitting deep ruts when well cranked over and screwing it hard, though this only happens when one's perhaps asking a little much from a machine loaded to the hilt, set up for long distance touring and being caned hard, when the rear end goes coil-bound.

Suspension is in the normal British tradition, taut and hard, perhaps not to quite the extent

continued over

NORTON
COMMANDO 25,000 miles on

practised by the Italians, but a far cry from most Japanese machines' characteristics. Minor road irregularities are transmitted straight through to the rider, while larger craters frequently require longer travel than is provided. Heavier riders may find the ride rather better, as matters improve immensely two up (10 stone rider, 8½ stone pillion) and the bike loses much of its "tip-toe" feeling. Taken all round, the suspension proves adequate for nearly all riding conditions, only the worst Continental potholes, crossed two up and heavily laden producing bottoming, but not actively comfortable.

Comfort could also be improved in the seating department, there being inadequate padding to cope with 300-mile plus runs without the old numb . . . , though Interstate and Roadster versions feature somewhat thicker foam. Overall riding position's reasonably good with the European bars fitted, a slight forward lean, footrests about right for my five foot eight inches, though taller riders usually complain they're too far forward, the penalty for non-adjustable pegs, and the foot controls are easily fitted to the individual's requirements.

Any machine's handling characteristics being to some extent a compromise between low speed comfort, soft and wallowy, and high speed stability, the Commando obviously opts for the top end of the spectrum. It's disappointing, therefore, to find that just when the discomfort of the low speed hardness should pay off in terms of rock steady high-speed handling, there's that nervous, twitchy feeling. However, the trick's to relax and *not* to fight it — all's OK once one accept the fact that there's nowt dangerous about it, but it does require getting used to, and doubtless explains the varied accounts of Commando handling.

Most of the braking action's provided by the front disc, hydraulically actuated by a handlebar mounted master cylinder. Fluid is pumped to the twin pistons in the heavily ribbed cast aluminium caliper unit bolted to the right-hand fork leg, applying the two circular disc pads to the cast-iron disc. Lever pressure's on the heavy side; it's thus easy to come to a finely controlled

gradual halt, with no risk of sudden wheel locking on nasty surfaces, although emergency retardation requires considerable effort.

However, under such conditions there's never any difficulty in obtaining maximum retardation, and it's always possible to lock the front wheel up under really hefty braking. One becomes rapidly used to the pressure required, the relationship between lever pressure and braking force being totally predictable, and this rider's never run out of brakes in nearly 25,000 miles of hectic riding, other than through brake failure, of which more anon. Pad wear, however, it extremely rapid in poor weather conditions, three sets of pads having been chewed through at approx 3,500 mile intervals, this increasing to a 10,000-15,000 mile life in rain free conditions. At £1.20 a set, it's no great expense, but a retrofit stainless steel wiper blade system is being introduced, and pad life should undoubtedly be greatly improved. The cast-iron disc, dull chromium plated, rusts at the slightest opportunity, and this surface rust is scattered all over the front end of the bike when the pads are subsequently applied.

Despite the excellent coefficient of friction afforded by cast iron, it's high time that an answer was found to this problem, and indeed stainless steel discs are rumoured to be on their way. Oval cross-sectioned front fork legs, massive spokes and a substantial spindle prevent fork twist under heavy braking, and this together with the grippy 4.10 x 19 TT100 boot enable full use to be made of the braking power. Maintenance is extremely simple, a clamp bolt and one nut securing the front wheel, whose removal enables pad changing to be accomplished in a couple of minutes. Pad wear can be checked without removing either wheel or caliper assembly, a task which must be accomplished regularly in wet weather as it has proved possible to eject pads under braking before the warning singing of metal to metal, disc on pad backing material, occurs — result no brake!

At the back, a 7 inch single leading shoe stopper is incorporated in the final drive sprocket. Operated by cable, it's an unex-

citing contributor to the overall braking. There's little or no risk of a clumsy hoof locking the rear end up under heavy braking, and its real use is limited to preventing the back from hopping around too much, and to coming to a gentle halt in traffic. The combined brake/chain wheel, allied to a system of paddles, enables the rear wheel, complete with transmission shock absorbing pads to be removed by merely withdrawing the rear wheel spindle ie one nut — at least, that's the theory, but the exhaust system gets in the way, so the silencer rubber bolts have to be disconnected, a further two nuts.

However, it's still a genuinely QD system, eliminating the need for realignment etc on replacement. Like the easy front wheel removal (necessary for frequent disc pad renewal) it's just as well the task's a doddle, as the plastic shock absorber inserts require inspection at 10,000 mile intervals, and believe me, at 10,000 mile intervals, they require replacement! Again, not expensive at £1.20 the set, or difficult to achieve, but a niggling annoyance, a poor substitute for a properly thought out, decently constructed shock absorber.

Rather on the heavy side, the clutch nevertheless can stand hefty abuse, and although long periods of clutch slipping like on rough tracks results in excessive lever clearance appearing, with subsequent drag, when cool normal clearances are restored. Plate wear in 25,000 miles is practically nil despite several attempts at burning the thing out, while the new all-metal clutch promises even longer life. Clutch dismantling can only be achieved with the aid of a diaphragm spring compressor, but as compensation there's no need to adjust springs to achieve parallel plate disengagement, thus effecting considerable maintenance time savings.

Adjustment is simplicity itself, a cap in the primary chaincase allowing access to the operating pushrod adjusting screw and locknut. Cable adjustment is at the handlebar end, and can be easily accomplished whilst on the move. The Achilles heel of the clutch department is the cable itself, exposure to foul weather rapidly converting a clutch already on the heavy side to a real bicep

developer, eventually resulting in nipple popping, the cable's that is! With no provision incorporated for oiling the cable, it's an unwelcome fag to strip out the cable, connect up lubricator, etc, etc, ad nauseam. Whilst appreciating that the incorporation of an oil nipple would doubtless add immeasurably to the factory's costs, it would result in far fewer complaints being directed at the clutch, although the current 850s include modifications to the withdrawal mechanism, lightening the actuating pressure.

Primary chain tensioning is achieved by checking through one of the aforementioned caps, then moving the gearbox back or forth by means of a draw bolt — sounds simple when you say it fast and indeed is, but for the location of the engine feed and return oil pipes, which effectively prevent a spanner being placed on the adjusting nuts! It's fortunate that the triplex chain rarely requires adjustment, perhaps every 5,000 miles, the final drive chain seemingly absorbing all the punishment. At 25,000 miles approximately half the gearbox adjustment has been utilised, and a primary chain life of 40-50,000 miles is thus entirely practicable. Rear chain is rather a different kettle o' haddock, 7,000 miles having proved about the limit, not bad by current standards, especially considering the relatively small dimensions of the Renold's unit, due doubtless to the frequently over-enthusiastic chain oiler fitted, which also protects the rear of the machine from any suspicion of rust, and effectively waterproofs pillion riders' boots.

This problem is intensified by the totally inadequate chain guard fitted, its straight top edge preventing any of the oil flung off by centrifugal force where the chain wraps itself round the final drive sprocket from being retained, though the Mk 1A 850s are slightly improved here — when, oh when, will we get away from these foul exposed rear chains? MZ, on machines costing around the £200 mark have shown everyone that a full enclosure chaincase can be simple, effective, and damn it all, actually *attractive*, unlike some of the rather heavy looking examples of the late 50s and early 60s.

The gearbox dates from the

21

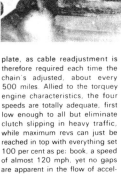

above period, but despite its white hairs performs as well as any. A little sensitive to clutch adjustment, chain tensions etc, cog swapping's a delight when all's in harmony, the clutch a superfluity once under way. Standard ratios are semi-close, revving the motor to 6,500 or 7,000 rpm in each gear before changing dropping the revs to 4,500-5,000, smack into the maximum torque band.

Overall gearing may be altered by swapping gearbox output sprockets, this necessitating the removal of the primary drive, a simple enough task providing a sprocket puller and the previously mentioned diaphragm spring compressor are available, but hardly encouraging frequent monkeying around — still, at least gearing can be altered, which is more than can be said for many machines. On the 21-tooth sprocket that's normally fitted on UK models, gearing's very slightly on the high side, max revs only being available in top with everything absolutely spot-on, but making for relaxed cruising, 90 mph representing 5,300 rpm. For the maximum practical acceleration for road use, a 19-tooth sprocket is fitted, but this limits top speed to around 108 mph, lowers the comfortable cruising speed and adds to tyre, fuel and chain bills.

All in all, the transmission is robust and pleasant to use, simple to maintain and theoretically easy to adjust, but it's spoilt by a lack of cable oiler, oil pipe obstruction of the primary chain adjustment mechanism, and rather irksome rear wheel adjusting screws. It's a pity that the rear brake outer cable stop is mounted on the swinging arm, rather than on the brake

plate, as cable readjustment is therefore required each time the chain's adjusted, about every 500 miles. Allied to the torquey engine characteristics, the four speeds are totally adequate, first low enough to all but eliminate clutch slipping in heavy traffic, while maximum revs can just be reached in top with everything set 100 per cent as per book, a speed of almost 120 mph, yet no gaps are apparent in the flow of acceleration through the cogs.

Long the subject of innumerable bitter jokes, the electrics of the Commando are 100 per cent Joe Lucas, with the exception of the battery, now a Yashua. Standard equipment is a resin encap-

sulated alternator, silicone rectifier and solid-state zener diode providing the charge side of the picture, a seven-inch headlamp with integral pilot bulb, stop/tail lamp, currently of immense proportions to comply with our Transatlantic friends' legislation, trafficators and instrument illumination all attempting to discharge the battery, aided by the twin point, twin 6-volt coil, ballast resistor ignition set-up. Controlling this little lot is a four-position switch, off and parking lights only allowing key withdrawal, ignition only and lights and ignition retaining the key.

Switching to lights and ignition brings a headlamp shell mounted

switch into the game. The usual left-hand Lucas handlebar switch flips from dip to main beam, with headlamp flasher button above and horn push below. A matching console on the right bar controls the indicators, one button killing the ignition, the other sitting idle at present, waiting for the long promised electric starter to be fitted!

The lights are all more than adequate, the optional Lucas QH 60/55 watt headlamp being a real beaut, punching out a great tunnel of pure white on main beam, with a fairly well defined dip pattern illuminating the kerb without provoking protests from
continued over

NORTON COMMANDO 25,000 miles on

other road users. An idiot light mounted in the headlamp shell warns of main beam, while matching ignition and trafficator lamps are also fitted. These are well chosen, being bright enough to see in all but the most brilliant sunshine, without being distracting at night. Brake light switches are fitted to both front and rear operating mechanisms, the rear a sprung-loaded plunger, the front a hydraulically operated one.

The generating system is simple but effective, having no moving parts but for the alternator rotor, and no bearing surfaces to wear. One complaint that can be directed here is the relatively low output of some 110 watts which prevents the running of a two-beam or second headlamp unless a large capacity battery, capable of sustaining a slight discharge for reasonable periods of time is substituted for the standard 7½ amp hour job. Another gripe is the quality of the twin leaded cable emerging from the encapsulating material of the stator. Subjected to considerable heat and continually splattering with hot oil, the cable rapidly becomes extremely brittle and great care must be taken should alternator removal be necessary to prevent cracking. This has been the case since Lucas introduced the bike alternator, back in the 50s, but in these days of advanced plastics technology there can surely no longer be any excuse for this sort of thing.

So far, the Lucas electrics have acquitted themselves well, being functionally excellent and reliable, but they're let down in the sparks department. The contact breaker unit has caused many a holed piston and burnt valve in the past, through timing slip due to mechanical wear, but Lucas have beefed up the unit and claim to have licked the problem. Having fitted Boyer's tranny ignition, it's not been possible to verify the claim, but general opinion is that there's justification for it, though matters could still be further improved. Timing, thanks to a built-in scale viewed through a cap in the primary chaincase, is simplicity itself, permitting stroboscope readings to be made in seconds.

Final moan must be regarding the awful, tatty after-thought of a wiring harness that's fitted, Lucas apparently supplying but one

loom, to also fit the Triumph Trident triples, so various wires are surplus to requirements on a twin pot motor left hanging loose, their ends "protected" by silly strips of insulating tape.

Returning to the bike as a whole, detail finish is poor, but for certain exceptions. The major engine castings are rough and ready sand castings, cheap and easy to alter it's true, but presenting a surface cratered like that of the moon on the cylinder head and barrels. Some, however, are nicely polished out, like tha chaincase outer and the fork legs, but even they have their rough spots where the buff couldn't reach, and certainly don't present the razor-sharp finish and consistency of die castings. Unlike most Japanese machines, the polished ally has no plastic coating to protect it from attack by the elements, OK if you're a Solvol freak, not so good if, like me, you believe that a bike should come up gleaming after but a sudsy wash and hose down.

However, there's therefore not the problem of removing peeling plastic once the coating breaks down, as inevitably it does. Paint and chrome, too, are delicate finishes on the Norton, exceptions being at the lower end and at the back where the copious chain oiler and blown back engine drips see to protection. Spoke and spoke nipples suffer terribly, being but cadmium plated as are most of the nuts and bolts, soon reduced to hideous rust. Only real praise that can go to the finish is offered to the glass-fibre ware, the tank, tail faring and side panels, this being of great thickness, has a lovely deep, smooth, colour impregnated surface and is nicely tidied up round the edges.

So how's it all behaved over some 25,000 miles? Well . . . we started with oil all over the right boot but 10 miles from picking it up — porous cylinder head casting, though how it wasn't picked up during the famous final road test given every bike leaving the factory I'll never know. Replacement was accomplished the next day, top marks to the factory's service department. Replaced under warranty were a number of components whose finish just disintegrated, notably the chromed fork stanchions, the flaking chrome then wearing out the fork oil seals. At 8,000 miles an exhaust valve burnt out, probably

my fault, setting too tight a tappet clearance.

At about about 11,000, the transmission shock absorbers packed up, then rear wheel spokes started to snap at regular intervals, and despite a rebuild, continue to do so today when travelling fast, two up and loaded. The kickstarter pawl then wore out at 14,000, at 18,000 the oil control rings called it a day and were replaced, and at 20,000 one of the main bearings threw in the towel. Add to that oil leaks here, there and everywhere, prop and centre stands breaking and sundry other minor niggles, and one could hardly accuse the Commando of being dull! Most of these faults were accelerated by the long, fast, heavily laden travelling being done, but under similar circumstances I very much doubt if say a Honda 750/4 would have suffered as badly.

Servicing wasn't neglected, although that too is required rather more often than I'd like, especially chain and Isolastic adjustments. Fuel consumption under such conditions varied between 40 and 50 mpg, pretty reasonable by current standards, and could be improved up to the 60s with careful riding. Even trying, I doubt if it's possible to get much below 40 to the gallon, one of the four stroke's advantages. Oil consumption, assuming rings and seals OK, worked out at around 1,000 mp pint, most of that going through the rear chain oiler.

In summing up the Commando one can best perhaps describe it as cheap and cheerful. Cheap in price (for these inflated days), cheap in finish, but also in consumables like tyres and chains, not as disastrously priced as some, nor so often required, and at least readily available. Cheerful too, when it's going — I still know of very, very few bikes that are as nice to ride as a properly set-up Commando, R90S, Honda 4 etc included, while the performance is as much as most can use. As a functional piece of machinery it's got some excellent points, but it's let down by silly faults, poor attention to detail, and poor quality finish. At current prices, it's probably a fair buy; after all, you can't afford to make a silk purse out of a sow's ear!

NORTON INTERSTATE

The 850 not just a good motorcycle — but an outstanding one

THE MEMORY of our unhappy ride to Cologne two years ago, when we seemed to spend much of the trip at odds with our Norton Interpol, is still very clear. The whole episode left relationships just a little strained between us and Norton and it took perhaps eighteen months for the dust to settle.

A chance meeting with Mike Jackson who has, among his many other tasks at Andover, responsibility for the Press bikes, gave us the chance to clear the air. He accepted that we could do nothing but write about the bike as we found it; and we accepted that the bike *was* supplied at short notice and was no more than a hack that had seen better days. This was back in June. "Look," said Mike, "why don't you take a Commando to the Cologne show this year and give us the chance to redeem ourselves." He thought for a minute. "We'll even supply the tow rope." He was grinning as he said it. We accepted on the spot. We would be only too happy for the Norton to come through with flying colours and we also wanted to go to the Cologne show. It would make a change to have a bike arranged three months before, and not three days, as we usually manage things.

True to Norton's word, the Norton was ready for collection when we telephoned Andover a week before the date. It was to be the Mk 11A 850 Interstate. Not new, far from it in fact, for it was the one used by Peter Kelly of *Motor Cycle* for a Land's End to John O'Groats trip in the summer. Peter Williams had also taken it to the continent and it showed just over 5,000 miles on the odometer. That was no bad thing for if the bike did have any little idiosyncracies, one of the two Peters would have found them by now.

There has been a breath of fresh air blowing through Norton-Triumph these last few months. A few staff changes had changed attitudes also, and, at last, we had the feeling that someone realised that all too often the general public's opinion of a machine was influenced by what they read in the technical press. It makes sense to ensure, then, that the bikes given to the press are

good examples rather than bad. There is nothing dishonest in that, indeed they would be fools if they did not. Certainly, when we ride a machine we try to bear in mind that it has been supplied by the manufacturer, and we expect it to be good.

The Norton had been prepared for a long ride. A spare clutch cable was taped in position, spare plugs and disc pads were in the tank bag and a spare fuse was taped to the frame. Only the fuse was needed, and that was not the Norton's fault. It was comforting, though, to know that someone was interested enough in the bike to take the trouble. Perhaps readers might think that we are making an unnecessary thing about what ought to be a perfectly normal situation. Believe us, it is not as usual as all that and we were gratified to find that the sole remaining British manufacturer could at last hold its own with "the rest". Also supplied was the excellent French luggage carrying equipment that was first shown at the Racing and Sporting Motorcycle Show earlier this year. A tank bag and two tank-side bags clipped to a skin stretched over the tank. A smaller, ugly, bag was permanently fixed on top, like a wart, the only blot on otherwise handsome equipment. Made in some sort of vinyl, it looked better than it was, for the finish was poor on our set. The design was brilliant, though. It held enough luggage for my wife and myself for the weekend (with the assistance of an old Craven top box that just happened to fit the carrier also supplied). This was used for maps and suchlike). My share was the wart on top. As a matter of interest, they are available in this country to special order, for the Interstate and /5 or /6 series BMWs, from Gus Kuhn at £35 or so a set.

The story of the Norton Commando must go right back to the 1940s, earlier if you want to compare it with the Edward Turner Triumphs. Introduced as a 500 it grew to 600, then 650 and, with the arrival of the Commando concept about six years ago, to a 750 before finally arriving at its present 850 c.c. capacity. Generally it is admitted, even at Nortons, that the design is getting towards the end of its useful life. Long in the tooth is an oft

heard term. By that token, BMWs are also in the same boat, for their design has been around since 1923! The problem with Norton is not so much that the basic design is old but that within the limits set by available tools and jigs, there is nowhere left to go to strengthen the motor to accept considerably increased power. That is not to imply that the present motor is going to fly apart at the first sign of hard work, more that we doubt if Norton will be upping it to a thousand!

Power. For the past five years it has been the god worshipped by nearly all manufacturers. Perhaps at last we can see an end to this trend for top speeds are down on many machines, as the emphasis shifts to a search for "cleaner" engines making less noise. Norton are at pains not to make any claim for maximum power for their machines, which is perhaps better than some of the fairy stories we hear, aided by having different "standards" for measuring the power. What they do say is that maximum torque is 56 ft lb at 5,000 r.p.m. with a "red line" on the tachometer at 7,000 r.p.m. giving a useful spread of power. Certainly one of the virtues of the Norton is its unhurried approach to travelling quickly.

They have been saying for years that the vertical twin has had its day, but still it retains its popularity. As well as Norton, Honda, Yamaha, Laverda and Bennelli make large capacity (500 c.c. or over) twins and one or two others make smaller ones. Vibration is the bugbear and various

Left: Venerable it may be, but the Norton parallel twin engine remains one of the best-looking motorcycle power units; and it produces as much power as most of the "opposition". Above: Photographed in Belgium. Opposite page: Excellent French-made luggage-carrying equipment as used on the journey to the Cologne show

walls are lubricated by mist from the big-end feed and valve gear, pushrods and followers and timing case by the residue from the rocker feed returning down the pushrod tunnels. A breather runs from the rear of the car crank case back to the oil tank and another breather vents the tank to air. The gearbox has its own separate $\frac{1}{4}$ pint reservoir.

The contact breaker assembly is housed, under a removable cover, at the front of the timing case with the contact braker unit being a taper fit on the end of the camshaft.

On the left-hand side of the engine we have a good old-fashioned primary chain case, the gearbox of course coming as a separate package. We think perhaps it is the only one remaining in this unit construction age. Removal of the cover, catching the oil as best you can as there is no drain plug, reveals the alternator rotor mounted on the left-hand end of the crankshaft and drive to the gearbox via a massive triplex clutch. It is possible to remove the engine sprocket/clutch/and primary drive chain as a unit, should replacement be necessary. Again the accent is on functional simplicity. The clutch is of the diaphragm type, and very pleasant it is too.

Now to the gearbox. Like the engine a classic in simplicity. It must remain as the last bastion of the four-speed school and, frankly, it is ample. Nortons have always been famous for their gearboxes, and this one is a superb example. Its only drawback was its much publicised inability to cope with the power under racing conditions. Among the advantages of having a separate gearbox is that of having its own oil reservoir, ensuring good, clean, comparatively cool oil all the time. This can mean less gear-change "stickiness" after a prolonged spell of high-speed work. And of course it can be hoisted out very

easily for repair jobs. Again the theme of simplicity.

The gears are in "extra-tough" nickel-chrome steel. The kickstarter drives through an internal ratchet on the layshaft first gear, which in turn drives the mainshaft and clutch. That is one of debits. If you stall it in traffic neutral has to be found before restarting.

The carburettors are Amal 932s, 32mm and, again with Triumph, have the distinction of being equipped with ticklers. They were needed, too. At least that's one less hole in the gloves to worry about if you are among the majority of riders without these (essential) items! One of the oft-heard complaints about the Commando is a tendency for the nuts holding the exhaust pipe to the head to come undone. Now they are securely retained by a locking washer and ours didn't budge. The pipes were blue when we took delivery of the machine, a common enough occurrence these days on most bikes.

methods are used to try to cancel it out. Norton, of course, use the much publicised Isolastic system wherey the engine and gearbox and exhaust systems are isolated from the cycle parts and rider by rubber mountings. That it works in most conditions there can be no doubt but, because the rubber has to be "tuned" to absorb the vibration at normal running speed, it is less effective at lower speeds, when it allows the engine to shake. That limit can be set by the designer without too much difficulty but if he moves it from one place he has to lose it from another. Norton have settled on a lower limit of 3,000 r.p.m. Below that the engine shakes considerably. It still does not transmit vibration as such to the rider, this is still absorbed, but he is very conscious of the movement of the engine and it is possible to feel it occasionally clunk against something solid down below. It seemed to be the inside of the left-hand alloy footrest casting. From 3,000 to the top of the scale there is not the slightest trace of vibration evident to the rider and within this range the Commando must rate as one of the smoothest motorcycles in the world.

The Norton engine has been much maligned over the past few years because it has not changed in basic design since the days of the Model 7. One thing is often overlooked when criticising it. Because the design is unchanging it has the real virtue of simplicity. It is a twin-cylinder parallel twin with pushrod-operated valves. In fact it is so simple that owners can actually decarbonise it in an afternoon! The cylinders have an alloy cylinder head and an iron barrel. Compression ratio is 8.5 to 1. Each piston has three rings, and no ring is used at the skirt of the piston. The pushrods run in tunnels cast in the barrel and operate the pistons by a conventional rocker arm. Valve closing is controlled by coil springs. Cylinder head removal can be accomplished with the engine in the frame.

At the bottom end the crankshaft, a hefty bolted up assembly, uses car-type big end shells, also bolted up, to house the connecting rods. Removal and replacement is a relatively simple operation. The camshaft, a single one being used to operate all four valves, is at the front of the engine with the drive by chain. The sprocket for this drive is on the right-hand end of the crankshaft and free play is taken up by a slipper tensioner. Behind the camshaft drive sprocket is the oil pump drive pinion, the oil pump being of gear type with a pressure release valve should the pressure rise above 45/55 lb/sq inch.

One of the less common features of the Norton is that, with Triumph, it uses a dry sump, the oil coming from a separate five pint tank under the dualseat. A replaceable filter is built into the return flow, accessable from behind the gearbox. Oil flows from the tank to the pump and from there by separate feeds to the big end, and main bearings and to the rocker spindles. Cylinder

Super Profile

The frame is of duplex-cradle type, twin down tubes looping under the engine and sweeping back up to meet the large-diameter top tube at the rear of the fuel tank. A secondary tube runs from the bottom of the steering head to just over half-way along the top tube. Two more tubes run from either side of the gearbox at the top mounting point to meet the top tube at much the same point as the secondary tube. No gusseting is used at all. The dualseat is supported by a sub-frame. The rear swinging-arm assembly pivots to the rear of the gearbox and the footrests, front and rear, are attached to a beautiful cast-alloy plate on either side.

Controversial from the day it was introduced, the Isolastic engine-mounting system has certainly had its fair share of press comment, favourable and otherwise. Norton feel that often it is blamed for other problems, i.e., incorrectly fitted or unsuitable tyres and they feel that, provided that it is set up by the book, it handles and performs as well as the best. The engine is "suspended" at three points, by a plate from the top of the cylinder head by two rubber mountings to the frame; by two bonded and two more rubber mountings at the bottom front of the engine, either side; and by three bonded and two rubber buffers above the gearbox, to complete a triangular mounting pattern. The whole essence of the system is that the shimming, i.e., play between the engine and frame, must be right. The ideal gap is given as 10 "thou". Too much play and the engine shakes in the frame, affecting handling — too little and vibration makes itself felt. The exhaust system remains in isolation with the engine by way of rubber mountings at its only point of contact with the frame, at the rear.

Front forks have the fashionable skinny look and the rear suspension units are adjustable Girlings, both conventional enough systems. Since we last tried a Commando the disc brake has arrived on Nortons, a well-made and effective unit by Lockheed offering a braking area of 18.69 sq. in. The drum rear brake gives an effective area of 13.60 sq. in. The wheels use Dunlop TT100s, 4.10 x 19 in. front and rear, with the rear wheel offering that most unusual asset, a genuine q.d. removal. Until 1971 the wheel was held to the brake drum by three studs which passed through the hub. Since then these have been replaced by polyurethane shock absorber segments which let into the hub. To remove the wheel all that needs to be done is remove the spindle, drop the speedometer drive housing and lift the wheel out. It is such an asset to have a q.d. rear wheel; it could well be enough to swing the balance towards the Norton if the prospective buyer were unable to make up his mind.

The petrol tank, finished in black and having "Norton" boldly emblazoned on the sides, held just under five gallons, an excellently large amount. As for the dualseat, that too earned high praise for it was still comfortable after 10 hours' riding. One last asset were mudguards made in stainless steel. Very nice.

Our look at the Norton has been more comprehensive than usual and, to our delight, the closer we looked the more there seemed to be to commend the bike. Half the battle when writing about a bike is won if the manufacturer helps the tester to understand it; Norton sent us not one but two comprehensive workshop manuals to peruse at our leisure. Most other manufacturers consider they are being generous if they give us a sales pamphlet! Such helpfulness gave us the chance to appreciate some of the features of the Commando, not least its classic simplicity. The

number of special tools needed to complete every major task on the bike is minimal and an enthusiastic owner would have no difficulty in acquiring the lot.

THE RIDE

Our normal practice is to report on a bike as we find it over a period of time but, in this case, we will just talk of one ride we had on the Commando, the aforementioned trip to Cologne.

Our trip to Cologne was to be as part of a club run, a dozen bikes meeting at Dover to journey to Germany. It could have been an interesting situation for the other 11 were all BMWs! As a BMW owner myself, I should have shrugged my shoulders and apologised for my thoughtless choice of transport (at least if I was conforming to the popular image of BMW owners). Almost to my surprise, I became defensive about the Norton. I had already covered a couple of hundred miles on the bike and was both astounded and overjoyed to find that I loved it. It suited me to perfection and I was determined that by the time we returned to England the Interstate would still be able to hold its head high.

To tell truth, it got off to a most unfortunate start for we had gone barely five miles when part of the headlamp glass fell out! A flying stone, presumably, had caused a freak break and there we were at eight o'clock at night with a hole in our light — and our timetable. Where were we going to get such a unit at that time of night? As luck would have it, we were directed to a late night accessories shop in Kennington, Stockwell Motors, where the man in charge, a motorcyclist, after much searching came up with a quartz halogen unit that was more or less the same as we needed. We breathed a sigh of relief that we were on one of the few bikes for which it was possible to get replacements late at night. Within an hour we were on our way to Dover and caught the midnight boat in good time.

By the time the ferry steamed into Ostend, at 4 a.m., a ghastly hour, we had discovered only one aspect of the Interstate that we didn't like. It needed one hell of a swing to start it. Eight hundred and twenty-eight fairly highly compressed c.c. shared out between two cylinders, and no valve lifter, is just too much and I am bound to say that starting the bike was never much fun. Especially at 4 a.m.!

The real surprise came from the Interstate the moment we heard it start. It was so quiet! Just about on a par with a BMW 900. They have really done things to the silencing arrangements on this bike. Mechanically it had barely a rattle, the air was effectively drowned by a new air cleaner system, and the silencers, with a black cap on the end (to pronounce death to noise?) were superb. Of course, there had to be a snag. Norton did not do this entirely out of concern for the ear drums of passers-by. Pending United States legislation gave them a hearty shove in the right direction and they came up with the goods. The price to be paid is a falling off in performance, with top speed reduced from a claimed 122 m.p.h. to a hard-to-find 110 m.p.h. For my money it matters not one whit, for who really cares about an extra 15 m.p.h. at that dizzy end of the scale? Let us hope that the paying customer takes the same view. The other effect is psychological. The Norton Interstate no longer makes a very "fast" noise. It never seems to be hurrying and bystanders, or pillion passengers, could be forgiven for thinking that it is a bit sluggish. Certainly its initial acceleration is a little down, now it is more content to make haste quietly. More power to its elbow; or rather not, for I'm very content with it the way it is.

Winding through Ostend streets before dawn meant that we could do so without being assailed by Belgian toots and in no time the bikes were pointing towards Brussels. I was last away and a prolonged spell of 90 m.p.h. cruising showed that the Interstate was very happy at that speed, and that it was damned chilly! Brussels came and went without our getting lost, thanks to the leader, whom we had now caught, knowing where he was going. Our destination was Stadtkyl, a village in the Eifel Mountains, a club meeting place and stopping-off spot for many riders at the Elephant Rally. After a stop for coffee and fuel, where a tankful showed that we were averaging 59 m.p.g., a figure that was to be repeated constantly, we completed the 200-odd miles to Stadtkyl just after most were leaving the breakfast table.

A couple of hours to try and remove the sand from our eyes and then a massive German lunch followed by a tour of some of the local beauty spots, the Commando behaving itself magnificently. Naturally, being in Germany, wherever we stopped it was the "foreign" bike

Is the Norton now unique in having an old-style separate gearbox (four-speed too, which is getting rare) with primary drive by chain? It's a setup that works very well, with several practical advantages

that caused most interest and I was genuinely happy that it still looked pristine. No oil was leaking and it sounded great. Starting wasn't getting any easier, though. It *started* well, to be fair. My only problem was to spin the engine. I usually settled for putting the bike on the centre stand and standing alongside. At least that way I reduced the chances of thumping my knee on the oil tank.

It was 50 miles from our village to Cologne, a pretty, sunny ride that was made more pleasurable by the company, increased later when the rider of a 250 NSU joined us. Arrival at Cologne coincided with countless thousands of other motorcyclists and there was a long, slow-moving queue into the exhibition hall where IFMA was being held. Not once did the Norton object and it was happy most of the time to plod along, clutch out, in bottom gear at about 2 m.p.h. I wouldn't have believed it. It was at variance with its tickover which, when stationary, had a tendency to increase to 2,000 r.p.m. where it normally would settle at a steady thousand.

It was dark when we returned to the mountains. And chilly too. The Norton's 60/55w lights were not as good as I recalled due, I later discovered, to a badly located bulb but the switches and control layout were excellent and I had become used to them. I wouldn't go so far as to say that I like the long-eared Lucas dipswitch/indicator switch but it worked and gave me no trouble, so perhaps I am allowing my initial dislike of them to linger unfairly.

More substantial German food and a glass or two of the magnificent local wine left us well armed to retrace our footsteps to Ostend the next day and we bade our German companions goodbye and once again enjoyed the trip through southern Belgium, passing the remains of the Siegfried Line just before we left Germany. Once again passports were not required, nor insurance, and we were delayed for only seconds. The more I rode the Norton the more I was enjoying it. It was still returning 59 m.p.g.; top speed, not outstanding at 110, was ample, more than ample in fact for *everywhere* seems to have speed limits these days, and the comfort was outstanding. Even the luggage equipment was playing a part by keeping the wind off my knees.

Sunday riding in Belgium was to be avoided, we were warned, but I am bound to say I much preferred it to the English equivalent. Not once were the Norton's excellent brakes called upon to work unduly hard. The squeak that they had from delivery was beginning to disappear and only in the wet did they worry me (as do *all* disc brakes). As we never had a drop of rain that was not a problem. The big engine was more than happy at the 80/85 m.p.h. that we tended to cruise at. This speed settled the tachometer needle to 5,000 r.p.m. and the sensation to the rider was that of sitting on a smooth, but icy, magic carpet. At that speed the miles were fast disappearing and we stopped just before Ostend for a meal, confident that there was no boat for hours. There was, of course, but enquiries beforehand had assured us otherwise.

The crossing was accomplished without incident, if one can ignore a Force 8 gale and, finally disembarking at Dover and going through the usual customs queues, we had a high-speed run to Surrey and arrived, after a very long day, with not an ache or twinge between us. I was still enjoying myself and could, happily, have gone on as long as I could keep my eyes open. The trip meter said that we had done just 720 miles in the last three days, hardly as far as Newcastle, but different, somehow. In that time I had not adjusted the chain (I hadn't needed to), the merest trace of oil leaked from the clutch cable entry to the gearbox and a drip came from the primary chaincase. Not a drop of oil was needed during the trip and no adjustments were made, excluding the headlight of course, and a blown fuse when we got our wires crossed in the dark replacing it.

As a long-distance touring motorcycle the Norton Interstate had shown itself to be ideal. The only detail criticism that could be made was regarding the ignition/light key mounted inaccessibly under the tank. Starting was, of course, always an irritation but in its defence I am afraid I will have to tell the story of how I took the Norton along to the local training scheme one Sunday morning and a slim young lady who is instructor there asked if she could have a ride. "Of course," I replied, "if you can start it." She did. First kick. Exit one tester with egg on his face. I forgot that she owned a 650

Triumph. That is the last time I take her to the TT in my sidecar.

Another aspect of the starting situation is that the long-promised starter motor is now nearing reality. One of the weeklies has carried a picture of it and an electric-starter equipped bike was reported as attending the FIM Rally in June. If it is man enough for the job, and Lord knows it ought to be, the time taken to develop it, it removes just about the last obstacle to the Norton breaking through as a top seller. In every other respect it is good. Its handling is steady at high speed, it goes around corners without twitches or complaint and it is light enough (430 lb) and has a short enough wheelbase (56¼in) to be able to be flicked through bends with more ease than its apparent bulk suggests. In fact, by today's standards, it is a lightweight, and most riders enthused over its typically British good looks. A handsome bike rather than a pretty one. The suggestion that it is a long-distance tourer is a considered one. The engine does not become really smooth until the bike is doing 50 m.p.h. (3,000 r.p.m.); riding around town was not unpleasant, just not much fun. Certainly a bike for the open road, and one to be ridden quickly.

One only needs to return to British tyres for a week or two to discover that there really is a difference between them and Japanese ones. We had no rain on the German trip but plenty after, and the bike was rock steady in the wet. Dunlop TT100s suit the Commando well.

Perhaps readers will consider that we have dwelled too long on the Norton's virtues and we, too, were a little surprised to find that we had so much to say about it. We did ask ourselves the question: How much of our enthusiasm for the Norton was genuine and how much was dictated by our desire to see it succeed? It would be an easy trap to fall into. Norton-Triumph are the last bastion of British motorcycling. Without them we have nothing. "So what, you may say. Look at it from the selfish point of view. Without Norton the home industry loses a valuable, indispensable, almost, buffer against the worst excesses of the politicians. The incentive to go easy on the motorcycle because we still make them and sell them abroad is removed. That matters to all of us. From an unselfish point of view, none of us wants to see the last rites administered to a once great national industry. Perhaps you, like us, love motorcycles and love the contribution that we have made to the worldwide development of it. Take Norton away and that contribution stops.

Certainly we were not unaware of the political considerations of Norton's success or failure but, with this in mind, we still came to the honest conclusion that the Norton Commando Interstate that we tried was not just a good motorcycle, it was an outstanding one. Now we are aware of the problem. Not *all* Nortons leave the production line as good as ours. Quality control is something that the Norton-Triumph management have to get to grips with before they can claim to be among the best in the world. When they do and all Nortons are up to the standard of the one that we have just returned to Andover they will have a winner. And we will be there cheering for it.   B.P.

OWNER'S VIEW

Although at one time I owned a plunger-sprung Model 7 Dominator twin of the type that can be regarded as the true ancestor of the Commando, my experience of the latter model has been limited to a series of short runs at the time when I was writing the *Norton Commando Owners Workshop Manual* for the Haynes Publishing Group. With such little first-hand experience I have had to rely heavily on comments from two local enthusiasts who own and ride Commandos, and from the experiences of a member of the local police force who has covered many thousands of miles on a 750cc Interpol in the course of his duties. Everyone to whom I have spoken has shown real affection for what is undoubtedly the last of the British-made 'Superbikes' – and perhaps the last of the four-strokes to be associated with the legendary 'Unapproachable' Norton, to use the once familiar trade mark. The reason for this is not hard to see, for any machine that managed to win the *Motor Cycle News* 'Machine of the Year' award for five successive years must be something special. To gain this accolade at the very time when the larger capacity Japanese machines were gaining wide acceptance in Britain makes this achievement all the more remarkable.

My first interview was with Pete Shoemark of Galhampton, Somerset, who acquired an early Fastback 750 about six years ago, having purchased it from a friend who was moving abroad. His comments make interesting reading, the more so because his machine is now undergoing a full-scale restoration:

JRC: Why are you so interested in the Norton Commando?
PS: To me, the Commando represents one of the best ever 'all purpose' machines. It is small and light enough to use for commuting, yet it will handle long, high-speed runs without complaint. It is remarkably frugal and is easy and cheap to maintain. Buying a Commando was a logical step from running various postwar British machines, as it combines most of the virtues with few of the vices.
JRC: When any why did you buy your Norton Commando?
PS: I bought it from a friend about six years ago, as it was a machine I had often wanted to own, and it came along at the right time and price. Commando prices were at their lowest about then, and have been rising slowly in recent years.
JRC: What condition was it in? If you found faults, were these common problems?
PS: The general condition was good, given that it had spent most of its life in London. My personal preference is for the Roadster model, so I converted my machine from its original Fastback specification. It is easy to change the tank and seat etc, but I took the precaution of retaining all the original parts so that the machine can be reconverted easily, if needs be. Faults were of a relatively minor nature. Being an early model, Wipac switches were fitted. I changed these for some second-hand Yamaha switches which are a great improvement. The automatic timing unit is worn, and in the future this will be replaced by Boyer electronic ignition. The carburetters are worn too, and I am working on

a single carburetter conversion.

Trying to keep the two carburetters in accurate synchronisation for any period of time seems to be a common problem with Commandos. Given that twin carburetters are mostly of cosmetic value on a road-going long-stroke parallel twin, a single carburetter seems the logical move to make. A very high quality 2 into 1 manifold was obtained for me from California, but I have yet to make the final choice of carburetter.
JRC: What repair/renovation work has been done and what advice would you give to someone facing the same problems? Would it have been an economic proposition to have bought a machine in better or worse condition than yours originally?
PS: Relatively few repairs have been necessary, apart from a complete gearbox rebuild. The load faces of every gear tooth were badly pitted, and I suspect much of this was due to condensation, which is a constant problem in the separate AMC gearbox. The gear oil soon becomes a white emulsion and should be changed very frequently. Another problem has been the support tube that carries the swinging arm pivot pin at the rear of the gearbox cradle. This tends to wear oval on the early models, so I have fitted stop bolts to provide correct location of the pin.

I am generally happy with the way in which things have gone with my machine. To anyone contemplating the purchase of a Commando I would suggest that, given a reasonable degree of mechanical competence, they find the cheapest, sound, runner that they can locate, and spend any surplus money on the cosmetics and detailing. As long as the machine is not conspicuously worn out, there will be few major problems. For advice, the Service Notes produced by the Norton Owners Club take a lot of beating.
JRC: Have you experienced

difficulty in obtaining any parts? What solutions did you find?

PS: Very few problems, apart from odd items like Isolastic buffer rubbers. In general, spares availability and prices will surprise owners of most 3 or 4 year old machines. Most pattern parts are of acceptable quality, but beware of some of the cheaper pattern reverse cone silencers. These are badly made, sound terrible, and stifle performance. If you don't know the difference, ask a knowledgeable owner who does, but as a general guide, don't buy a reverse cone silencer that you can't see right through.

JRC: What kind of performance and handling does your machine have?

PS: In terms of bhp, the Commando is not remarkable by modern standards. What it does have is large amounts of torque. Given that it is very light compared with most machines of similar displacement, it is pleasingly quick. It is almost perfect for twisty A and B roads, but if you require fast motorway cruising, don't buy a Commando.

Handling has often been compared unfavourably with the 'featherbed' Nortons — my reply would be that it lacks the fine edge that my Ducati has, but will still run rings round the majority of modern machines. Viewed in current day terms, it may lack comfort, but little else. It is, of course, important to keep the Isolastic adjustment at, or a little below, the maker's limits.

JRC: Is your machine in regular use? How practical is it? Are the running costs high?

PS: My Commando is currently undergoing a rebuild — mostly to improve the cosmetics. Prior to this it was used regularly for riding to and from work, and for longer runs at weekends. It never lets me down and will tolerate an amazing amount of neglect. If badly set up, it will run roughly, but it does run. Costs of running are very low — fuel consumption, for example, is between 60 and 70mpg.

JRC: Are there any owners' clubs or clubs that cater specially for the Commando? If so, how helpful is it to be a member.

PS: The Norton Owners Club is reckoned to be very good indeed, but I must confess to have failed to get around to becoming a member. For some inexplicable reason, none of the local riders seem to be club members, but most of them know one another quite well — almost like an unofficial club if you like.

JRC: Is there a specialist whom you have found particularly helpful?

PS: I have used a number of Norton specialists over the years, and all have been very helpful. It would be unfair to pick out any individuals, though, and I would refer owners to the classified section of the motorcycle newspapers and magazines.

JRC: How much enjoyment do you get from your machine?

PS: A great deal. It is acceptably fast and fun to ride. It is one of the few machines I can use to pop in to the shops or take on a 150 mile ride, without thinking twice. An unusually good all-rounder.

JRC: What advice would you give to potential Commando owners?

PS: Start by talking to as many Commando owners as possible. Most will be happy to discuss their machines and will be able to offer sound, practical advice on the choice of model. Take note of the inevitable accounts of weak and strong points, but do not treat these as infallible. As an example, the original parallel roller drive side main bearing has always been notorious as a potential source of trouble and, by reputation, must be replaced by the later 'Superblend' type. I would not argue against this, but my own machine has run happily since 1969 with the original bearings.

If changing from a modern four cylinder machine to a Commando, expect a degree of culture shock! The initial impression may be that the Norton seems crude and unsophisticated, its virtues being rather more subtle so that they will take more time to become apparent. Like many other European machines, the Commando has often been said to have 'character'. This is a very vague term which can mean many things to different people. To the mechanically-minded, the Commando will give a feeling of simplicity and longevity — that of a machine which can be kept running indefinitely. It does not have a useful working life as such, but will last as long as the owner wants it to. Conversely, if the intention is to ride hard and fast for a couple of years, with infrequent trips to a dealer for servicing, the Commando is best forgotten.

Like any other machine, the Commando has its weak points, and it is advisable to take along someone who knows the model when about to buy one. The main points to look out for are excessive play in the swinging arm, which can indicate ovality of the cross tube which carries the pivot pin, and a low pitched whine from the gearbox, which usually means a worn layshaft sleeve gear. Clutch slip under load is common on the early models, unless they have been fitted with the later sintered metal plates and hardened clutch centre. Exhaust port threads will wear rapidly if the flange nuts have not been secured correctly, and to effect a permanent repair the cylinder head must be removed to permit argon arc welding of dural inserts. As an alternative, Helicoil inserts can be fitted, without the need for dismantling.

Chris Rogers, of Milborne Port, Dorset, is another enthusiastic Commando owner who has one of the 850cc models made during the pre-Electric Start era. From the cosmetic viewpoint, his machine had been well looked after by the previous owner, as the accompanying photographs show. But there were signs that he did not have a similar appreciation of the mechanics of the machine, as the following comments show:

JRC: Why are you so interested in the Norton Commando?

CR: My interest in the Commando developed from the time the machine came into my ownership. I've found it to be a good, all-purpose motorcycle, which has been refined to a point where most of the mechanical problems inherent in the make have been eliminated. This has so far given me a high percentage of riding time in relation to the time spent on maintenance tasks, which obviously is ideal. I've found the finish of my particular machine to be very good, with practical features such as the fitting of stainless steel mudguards, which can only add to its longevity. All told, I've found the Commando to be a very enjoyable machine to ride, with no problems in handling and roadholding, and one that is relatively easy to maintain, given a common sense approach.

JRC: When and why did you buy your Norton Commando?

CR: It was purchased from a local garage during April 1982. It was spotted by a lady friend of mine who frequented the garage and who was acquainted with the garage owner. Upon enquiring if the machine was for sale, she was told that it was his private property and that he had been thinking about selling it for some time, but he had only just seriously considered advertising it in the local newspaper.

Described to me as being 'very nice looking and British' I was persuaded to visit the garage and view what turned out to be an 850cc Commando Mk 2A Roadster in very good and original condition. Previously, I hadn't considered anything other than Triumph twins, but after long and involved discussion with Pete Shoemark, a fellow author, and much bartering with the garage owner, I took the plunge and bought the machine.

JRC: What condition was it in? If you found faults, were these common problems?

CR: The general condition of the machine was very good. It had been ridden a reasonable amount, usually over moderate distances and in the dry. It was obvious that it had been cleaned frequently and had been stored in dry conditions on a showroom floor adjacent to some vintage machinery. A new Renolds chain had been fitted along with a new, pattern, silencer to replace the original component that had rotted out.

All of the faults that came to light during the months of familiarisation were purely mechanical and appeared, to the greater extent, to have been caused by lack of machine use and the unfamiliarity of the owner with the requirements for the maintenance of a British motorcycle. For example, it was found impossible to set the contact breaker gaps accurately and hence arrive at the correct ignition timing, as the original Lucas equipment was found to be well worn and quite badly damaged. In an attempt to compensate for the inaccuracy in timing, the carburetters had been set well out of synchronisation. I was amazed that the machine had run as well as it did.

JRC: What repair/renovation work has been done and what advice would you give someone facing the same problems? Would it have been an economic proposition to have bought a machine in better or worse condition that yours originally?

CR: Because the machine was in such good condition when purchased, my repair and renovation work has been minimal. Any alterations to specification have been made on grounds of improved efficiency and ease of maintenance.

The first item to be replaced was the air filter assembly. After the harrowing experience of trying to extract the element casing without removing most of the paint from the adjacent frame tubes, I decided to try and find a more compact one-piece filter unit. The ideal replacement proved to be one of K & N manufacture, no rejetting of the carburetters being necessary to compensate for this change in specification. Furthermore, the problem of having to purchase replacement filter-to-carburetter rubber bellows due to splitting was eliminated at the same time.

The damaged and inefficient contact breaker assembly was replaced, in the space of one afternoon, with a Boyer Bransden electronic ignition system. With the ignition timing correctly set, an improvement in engine performance was immediately apparent.

Before using vacuum gauges to check the carburetters for synchronisation, I decided to clean and service each carburetter. I found the throttle slides to be moderately worn, but I decided against replacement on the grounds that at some time in the future I hope to fit a single SU carburetter conversion. The throttle cable outer was found to be damaged due to incorrect routing, so this was renewed. Whilst doing this, I decided to dispense with the air choke arrangement, having been informed previously that it served no useful purpose. No problems have been experienced with the state of the engine tune since all this work was carried out.

To cure what was thought to be excessive vibration from the engine at speeds in excess of 50mph, I checked the Isolastic system. Whilst doing this, I found the protective gaiters of the front Isolastic mounting had split around their periphery and allowed water and road grit into the mounting. The component parts of the mounting were removed and cleaned, and to reset the shim clearance, I removed the complete mounting from the bike and supported it in a vice. No problems have since been experienced with the Isolastic system.

The fitting of gaiters to the front fork legs has been the one really major undertaking since the purchase of the Commando. This was necessitated by the seepage of fork oil past the top seal of one of the fork legs. Before fitting each fork leg with its gaiter, both bushes and the oil seal in each leg were renewed. The rapidly deteriorating aluminium painted finish of each fork yoke was rubbed down and degreased before applying two thick coats of a special matt black zinc-based paint which, to my mind, looks far superior to the original finish.

The stanchion of the left-hand fork leg was found to be badly worn at its contact area with the upper bush of the fork leg, but only for approximately one eighth of its periphery. This is no doubt the result of the twisting forces imposed on it through heavy braking; the stanchion was therefore turned through 90° before refitting it into the fork yokes. Fork action has been vastly improved by the rebuilding of the fork legs.

With the experience gained on the machine so far, I wouldn't be too hesitant in buying a Commando in poor condition, as replacement parts seem to be easily obtainable and the machine is mechanically quite simple. The main consideration would be the amount of time available to spend on the machine.
JRC: Have you experienced difficulty in obtaining any parts? What solutions did you find?
CR: I have experienced no difficulty whatsoever in obtaining parts for my Commando. I have always dealt with Ridge Farrant Motorcycles of Gosport, Hants, who provide an excellent service by return of post and who have the contacts to trace any item they may not have in stock.
JRC: What kind of performance and handling does the machine have?
CR: I think that machine performance should be judged in terms of what the rider really wants from the machine. To have a machine which will cruise at the legal motorway speed limit in an easy and relaxed manner with no problems of vibration or stress when loaded two up, with luggage,

is, so far as I am concerned, perfectly adequate. For the same machine to be an excellent country lane 'scratcher' with enough power to take it past the 'ton' would seem to be an excellent bonus. Machine handling is now very good, although some problems were experienced with ineffective front forks and incorrectly set Isolastic mounts, which have now been cured, as described earlier.
JRC: Is your machine in regular use? How practical is it? As the running costs high?

CR: I ride my Commando as frequently as possible, averaging throughout the year three to four days a week. A BSA B25SS is used for most of the remaining journeys, when it is necessary to ride through the rather hazardous road conditions that floods and the moving of farm equipment from field to field cause locally.

Obvious limitations on the distance that can be covered between stops for fuel are imposed by the small capacity tank fitted to the Roadster version of the Commando, this distance being no more than 120 miles. I am at this moment tackling the problem of fitting a larger capacity tank to the machine without altering its basic character. I feel that the fitting of a larger tank in conjunction with narrower handlebars will help to improve the riding position, as this is hardly satisfactory above 65mph, when wind pressure makes riding somewhat uncomfortable. I've found the average fuel consumption of 50mpg to be rather disappointing, as I've been told 750cc models in standard tune being able to average nearer 60mpg. 10mpg seems to be a high price to pay for a capacity increase of 83cc, although to be fair one pattern silencer on the machine may be adversely affecting its performance.

Of late, running costs have been confined to the normal requirements of fuel, lubricants, a new rear tyre and a set of sparking plugs. The engine uses very little oil

and most of this is lost through the inefficient seal between the tachometer drive cable and the crankcase. It was a pleasant surprise to find the rear wheel was of the quickly detachable type when it came to removing the wheel for tyre changing.
JRC: Are there any owners clubs or clubs that cater specially for the Commando?
CR: The Norton Owners Club, of which I am not a member.
JRC: Is there a specialist whom you have found particularly helpful?
CR: Not a specialist as such, but a maintainer of Triumph, Norton and BSA machines and a stockist of spare parts for later models of these makes. I refer to Pete Rogers, of Ridge Farrant Motorcycles, Whitworth Road, Gosport, Hants, whom I mentioned earlier.
JRC: How much enjoyment do you get from your machine?
CR: A great deal!
JRC: What advice would you give to potential Commando owners?
CR: Take great care when first viewing a machine. Generally, the Commando is very well finished and with some degree of regular maintenance and care it should stand up well to the ravages of use and time. If the machine being viewed shows signs of neglect, I should either beat the owner down to a rock bottom price or look elsewhere. I would not consider the Commando to be a collector's machine and there are plenty of good examples advertised in the motorcycle weeklies.

If my own Commando is a good example, an engine that is correctly set up should start on the first or second swing of the kickstarter, even if it is cold. With the engine running on tickover, listen for excessive mechanical noise from the timing chain area. I had to retension this chain and it turned out to be a long and involved job which necessitated draining the engine oil, removal of the contact breaker assembly and retiming the ignition. Except on the later Mark 3 850, there is no provision for checking the timing chain adjustment without first removing the timing cover. Check also for any severe snatch in the transmission and any related abnormal engine or gearbox noise. Commandos are known for giving the final drive chain a hard time, but the triplex primary chain should have a long life. Gearbox oil finding its way along the mainshaft and into the clutch, thereby causing some sticking of the clutch, is a common problem.

To give the gearbox any chance of an appreciably long life, its oil should be changed at regular intervals. To a lesser extent, this applies also to the engine. Question the owner closely as to whether oil changes have been carried out regularly and also determine the last occasion on which the oil filter was changed.

Correct adjustment of the Isolastic mountings and excessive wear in the bearings of the swinging arm pivot will be immediately obvious to the experienced Commando rider. The Isolastic mountings can, of course, be adjusted to suit rider preference, but Commandos have problems in the swinging arm fork pivot bearings, so check these bearings for wear with some care.

The points I have mentioned I would look out for specially, in the light of my own experience. But all the other checks appertaining to the purchase of any second-hand machine should also be carried out.

These two interviews sum up well what one can expect when contemplating the purchase of a Commando for the first time. But before closing this section of the book it will, perhaps, prove advantageous to take into account the way in which these machines were regarded by the police, who covered many thousands of miles on patrol and other duties. The machines with which they were supplied had been specially adapted for police work, the essential differences being the

fitting of two-way radio equipment, which in turn necessitated the fitting of a special high output generator, and a speedometer of certified accuracy. Known as the Interpol, these machines were finished in a distinctive white, and for anyone interested in the story of their development, details are given in the book A Million Miles Ago *by Neale Shilton (Foulis/Haynes 1982).*

When the first Interpol models were delivered to the Avon and Somerset Constabulary, they were to replace the 650cc Triumph Saint, a machine that had already established quite a reputation for itself. With its extra capacity, the 750cc Interpol was very well received, mainly on account of its much firmer handling characteristics and the amazing torque of the engine. The acceleration in third gear was particularly impressive, and this was to become an outstanding feature in pursuit activities that was the more appreciated after the force had changed to five-speed BMWs. No problems seem to have been experienced with the Isolastic system, most relating to main bearings and the persistent breaking of clutch cables due to the somewhat heavy operation caused by the use of a diaphragm clutch. This latter problem became quite serious when it was necessary to ride at slow speeds, such as when accompanying a wide load. The somewhat high bottom gear necessitated slipping the clutch, which then placed quite a strain on the cable. A secondary problem was attributed to mounting the carburetters directly on the engine. At low speeds, engine shake caused frothing in the carburetter float chambers, with the result that the engine would run very erratically at low speeds after the first minute or so.

Other problems encountered with the Interpol are characteristic of those found on Commando models in general — crankshaft failure until the change was made to barrel-shaped main bearings that would permit some flexure of the crankshaft, and broken exhaust pipe collars and stripped exhaust port threads, allied with inadequate mountings for the exhaust pipes. Yet despite these problems, all of which did not necessarily occur with every Interpol, my informant liked his Interpol and only began to realise some of its better qualities when he changed over to a 750cc BMW. But he is first and foremost a real motorcycle enthusiast, who always treats his machines with care and consideration. As a result, he probably had less trouble with his machine than the majority of the others that were used by Police forces all over the country.

It was the high maintenance costs that finally finished the Interpol; these being approximately three times those of maintaining the Triumphs used previously. It was for this reason, more than anything else, that a change was made to BMWs, with a drastic reduction in maintenance costs to something like half that of the Triumphs. But the change over to BMWs had its problems too, apart from the need to re-train the workshop personnel and re-stock with spare parts. There was the political issue of purchasing foreign machines as distinct from those made by the ailing British motorcycle industry who needed every sale they could get to ensure survival.

BUYING

During the period of almost 10 years, which represents the complete production span of the Norton Commando, it seems reasonable to expect that in excess of 50,000 models left the works. Taking into account the fact that the Commando is still too young to have qualified for a collector's value, there should be little difficulty in acquiring a suitable machine from a quite wide variety of sources at a reasonable price. Reference to the weekly motorcycling newspapers or the advertisements in the monthly magazines will give a good indication of the 'going rate' and what can be expected in general terms of value for money.

As can be verified from reference to the 'Owners' Views' section of this book, the Commando suffers from relatively few faults and even where these still exist, there is no real difficulty in obtaining the correct replacement parts or even alternative parts which, in some cases, will actually prove beneficial, assuming the owner has no wish to keep strictly to the original specification. In the main, these faults are main bearing problems, especially after extended use, excessive play in the swinging arm pivot pin housing, and difficulty in obtaining the correct ignition timing with the original contact breaker assembly. The other problems, such as keeping the carburetters in synchronisation and preventing the exhaust pipe nuts from working loose in the cylinder head, can be checked and controlled by regular, routine maintenance.

It is questionable at this time whether it is worthwhile restoring an early 750cc model to its original specification, in view of the fact that even after restoration the machine is likely to have little more than the current market value for any of the 750cc models. Still only 15 years old at the most, the Commando has a further ten years to go before it would become acceptable under the 25 year old rule of the Vintage M.C.C. – and even the likelihood of this rule continuing in the future is under discussion, due to the flood of late models that has tended to swamp the club in recent years. Yet for all this, the Commando represents a very practical way of obtaining and running an older machine at relatively low cost, if the prospective owner seeks something different from the general run-of-the-mill Japanese and other machines of foreign manufacture to be seen on our roads today. It becomes fun to run the machine for just what it is, being aware of its limitations but at the same time being assured of its reliability, good road manners and the ability to accept almost any kind of work short of sustained, very high, long distance speeds.

The question of whether or not to buy a cheap machine that is in need of complete renovation is one that is not easy to answer, because a machine that is nice-looking cosmetically can often prove just as expensive to recondition if major engine and gearbox components need to be renewed. There is never any guarantee that the previous owner's standards are similar to those of the prospective purchaser, so that what may seem acceptable to one may not be acceptable to the other. By rebuilding the machine completely from scratch, its overall condition will be known, and much experience gained that can be put to good use in the future. The only qualities needed are those of time, enthusiasm and good working conditions, together with the necessary tools and experience. Spares are unlikely to give rise to any problems, or even heavy expenditure, provided the correct contacts are made.

Of all the Commando models manufactured, it is to be expected that those made in the smallest numbers are likely to have the best chances of appreciating in value as time progresses. First and foremost amongst these is the John Player Replica model, which was manufactured for less than a year. Readily distinguishable on account of its white-painted fairing with red, white and blue flashes along both sides, and the twin headlamps, it has already become a quite rare sight on the roads today. Almost as rare is the 750cc Production Racer, which is street legal and capable of providing a much higher standard of performance that the equivalent 750cc standard production model. The 750cc Racer is equally rare, but at this was supplied in full race trim and without lighting, it would require a certain amount of modification to meet legal requirements for normal road use.

The later Electric Start models also have a certain amount of interest about them, if only because they represent the final phase of Norton Commando development. But it is wise to expect to have to use the kickstarter whenever the engine is cold, as the starter motor was never man enough for the job in hand, even with a new, fully-charged battery fitted. The fact that it is referred to euphemistically as an 'electrical assister' by those who are in the know explains all, for this is exactly how it was described unofficially by the works personnel. Anyone who has tried to start a Norton Atlas from cold, in below zero temperatures, will know exactly what kind of problem confronts the starter. Even so, some of these so-called Mark 3 850cc models looked very attractive, especially those finished in the traditional Norton black and silver finish.

I suspect almost every Commando owner takes delight in the machine's general handling capabilities, which make riding a pleasure and give an in-built feeling of safety without causing restraint of the throttle hand. Call it character or whatever else you wish, one has to admit there is still a great deal to be said for the standards originally established by the British-made motorcycle and upheld by them for so long. The Commando will make sure these qualities do not become forgotten as the years progress and other, more dubious standards, take their place under the guise of advancing technology.

CLUBS, SPECIALISTS & BOOKS

Clubs

Although there is no club that caters specifically for Norton Commando owners, the **Norton Owners Club** has much to offer that will make membership an attractive proposition for owners of these machines. With a membership in excess of 3000, and with a worldwide coverage, the club has 35 branches which form centrepoints for members to talk to each other, help out with machine problems, and to take part in various social events, rallies and branch runs. Amongst the many membership facilities is the ability to obtain spare parts at discount from a variety of dealers, and to participate in the club's spare parts scheme. Part of the membership subscription is used to underwrite this scheme, which is vital if Norton machines are to be kept on the road. Another portion of the membership subscription gives members the opportunity of joining an Emergency Aid/Friendship Scheme, with the aim of being able to effect repairs locally when a breakdown occurs during a journey, or just as a means of making contact with other NOC members. Like all the other services mentioned, this scheme operates on a worldwide basis and communication is aided by the club

magazine *Roadholder* which is published bi-monthly and contains a wealth of information as well as advertisements and news about the club in general.

Although the club caters for all Norton models, ranging from the sidevalve 16H to the Manx racing models, Commando owners are by no means overlooked. In 1979 the club published a particularly useful booklet entitled *Commando Service Notes* which was compiled and updated over a period of time by two particularly well-known ex-factory personnel, with a wealth of service experience between them. It would be fair to say that if a Commando owner does not have a copy of the booklet, his chances of trouble-free, long-life motorcycling, will be greatly diminished.

Enquiries about club membership should be made to:

John Evans,
'Polgath'
Commercial Street,
Cheltenham,
Gloucestershire, England.

Copies of *Commando Service Notes* can be obtained from:

Mrs. Jill Brown,
16, Green Park,
Cambridge, England.
(0223 65735)

Club members will, of course, be able to obtain copies of this publication at a preferential rate. It is an interesting fact that by far the largest proportion of club members are Commando owners.

Specialists

As may be expected, the Norton Owners Club, quite apart from its own scheme, has done much to ensure spares are still readily available. The club scheme is run by Les Emery who, due to the high level of demand, gave up his job with Lucas to open a shop selling these spares. In addition to selling

the club spares to *bona fide* club members, he also stocks other spares, and therefore forms a valuable point of contact. Having retained his seat on the NOC National Committee, Les is well placed to keep abreast of owners' problems, both from within the club and from those who patronise his shop. He has also manufactured many Norvil competition parts, as well as other parts for which there appears to be a market. A keen pricing campaign has enabled him to peg prices for much longer than others and even now he can more than match the prices quoted by other Norton spares sources. The address to contact is:

Fair Spares,
37, Albion Street,
Rugeley,
Staffordshire, England.
(08894 3974)

Other sources of spares are:

Mick Hemmings Motorcycles,
36/42, Wellington Street,
Northampton, England.
(0604 38505)

TMS Motors,
92-94, Carlton Road,
Nottingham, England.
(0602 53447)

R.G.M. Motors,
206-8, Rectory Road,
Bensham,
Gateshead,
Tyne and Wear,
NE8 4RR, England.
(0632 784460)

Gander and Gray,
592-594, Romford Road,
Manor Park,
London,
E12 5AF, England.
(01-478 6062)

Books

Until now, no book has been published that relates specifically to the Norton Commando, although reference is made to the various Commando models in each of the following titles:

Norton Twins by Roy Bacon. Published 1981 by Osprey Publishing Limited.

Norton by Dennis Howard. Published 1972 by Ballantine Books Inc, now out-of-print.

Norton Story by Bob Holliday. Published 1972 by Patrick Stephens Limited and subsequently revised.

For those who require more technical information, the **Norton Commando Twins Owners Workshop Manual** is still in print and available from the Haynes Publishing Group. It covers all models from 1967 to the end of production during 1977 and was produced with the full co-operation of NVT Motorcycles of Andover.

See 'Clubs' section for details of the publication **Commando Service Notes.**

PHOTO GALLERY

1. The so-called 'green-blob' Norton Commando, the original pre-production model displayed at the 1967 Earls Court Show. It was finished in silver, with an orange dualseat, the convex green blob on the petrol tank representing the new corporate image to be used by the manufacturer. (Motorcycle Sport).

2. Shaw Taylor, famous for his 'Police 5' series on ITV, visited the Norton factory at Andover for a Thames Television feature. Dennis Poore is seen in the foreground, seated on a conveniently-placed tea chest. (Mike Jackson).

3. This early 750cc Commando is of the post-'green blob' design era, as denoted by the absence of the extended 'ears' from the dualseat and the rear seat fairing. It is one of the coloured models and carries only a simple Norton transfer on the petrol tank. (Mike Jackson).

4. The twin leading shoe front brake used on the 750cc models is well ventilated by means of an air scoop. The brake operating mechanism and adjusters are on the right-hand side of the hub.

5. The left-hand side of the brake drum presents a very clean appearance with its domed outer cover.

6. Unlike the later models, the ignition key of 750 models fits into the forward-facing side of the left-hand side cover. The switch also controls the lights.

7. The twin Amal Concentric carburetters feed into finned, curved inlet tracts to give a semi-downdraught effect. The carburetter intakes are connected to the air cleaner box by means of rubber bellows which often perish and split.

2

3

4

5

6

7

8

9

10

11

12

13

8. A rotary disc valve breather is driven from the left-hand end of the camshaft. Note the front Isolastic engine mounting, adjustable by means of shims – these mountings were of a harder rubber compound on early machines.

9. The long footrest hangers are bolted to alloy plates. Each is curved, to give clearance to the primary chaincase and the kickstarter.

10. The full width rear hub has its end cover permanently removed on this machine, to provide better access to the long bolts that retain the quickly detachable rear wheel to the brake drum and rear wheel sprocket.

11. Early models have the characteristic moulded fibreglass 'Fastback' to smooth off the end of the dualseat. The pillion passenger grab rail is not a standard fitting. Circular reflectors were originally fitted in its place.

12. The type of silencer fitted is similar to that used for the earlier Norton Dominator twins, such as the Model 99.

13. The matching instruments of this 750 have the 'green-blob' Norton logo on their faces and are mounted within chromium-plated outer cases.

14

15

16

17

14. The rear drum brake is cable-operated and utilises a lug on the left-hand footrest hanger for the pivot of the operating pedal.

15. The rear suspension units of the early 750 are long and thin compared with those fitted to most other large capacity machines. Of Girling manufacture, they are adjustable in three different positions to suit load carrying and general riding conditions.

16. The forward portion of the dualseat extends on each side of the petrol tank to mask an ugly gap. Unfortunately the extensions are too short to be of use as knee grips.

17. This general view of the 750cc model owned by Mike Taverner of Chippenham, a member of the Norton Owners Club, shows several deviations from the original maker's specification. These include the headlamp mountings and the missing front mudguard stay, apart from the grab rail and the missing hub cover, already mentioned.

18. This later version of the 750cc Commando shows the 10.7 inch hydraulically-operated front disc brake and a change to traditional black finish, with the Norton transfer and lining in gold. (Mike Jackson).

19. The early 850cc models used this reverse cone type of silencer, attached to the upswept ends of the exhaust pipes.

18

19

20. There is no need to remove the hub end cover on the later models because the rear wheel can be detached quickly without need to remove bolts. A system using vanes and cush drive rubber buffers provided a much more satisfactory alternative.

21. The four-speed gearbox is of AMC design and was used throughout the entire Commando production run. It needs frequent oil changes to keep it in first class order.

22. The early 850cc models used a front wheel disc brake with the caliper mounted immediately behind the right-hand fork leg.

23. Side reflectors were mounted just below the steering head, immediately under the nose of the petrol tank. Note the twin ignition coils.

24. This machine has non-standard air cleaners, a modification carried out by many owners to prevent the constant splitting of the rubber bellows that join the air cleaner box to the carburetter intakes.

25. The earlier 850cc models retained the rear drum brake and its cable operation.

26. The headlamp now has three warning lamps in its shell, as well as the flick switch for changing from main headlamp bulb to parking light.

27

28

30

29

32

27. The all-black petrol tank, relieved only by the gold Norton logo and a thin gold line follows characteristic British practice. Ideally, for touring purposes, the capacity needs to be greater.

28. The engine kill button and the flashing indicator switch are contained in the assembly close to the twist grip, the extra button being unused except on the later Electric Start models.

29. The handlebars fitted to the Roadster model give a somewhat 'high rise' appearance, though not as much as those fitted to the American specification models.

30. The 850 dualseat has lost the 'Fastback' tailpiece of earlier models but has an integral grab rail. By this time the seat was much thicker in section and had a quilted top. Note the larger lens area of the rear light assembly.

31. The side covers used on the 850cc models are not quite so long as those of the 750 and tend to blend in better with the lines of the machine.

32. The rear suspension units no longer have protective shrouds, following racing practice. In consequence the exposed springs are chromium-plated.

31

33. The 850cc John Player Replica on display at the Milan Show in its distinctive livery and sporting the twin headlamps that afford instant head-on recognition. This model is now relatively rare and should acquire a collector's value. (Mike Jackson).

34. This photograph of a 1975 850cc Mark 3 Commando Roadster is of the Electric Start model fitted with the 10.7 inch rear disc brake. It appears to have been finished in John Player livery. Note the Japanese style mirrors, indicator lamps and absorption type silencers. (Mike Jackson).

35. The 850cc Mark 3A Electric Start model represents the last of the line and was in production for just over 2½ years.

36. This particular Interstate model was one of the last batch to leave Wolverhampton. As it has the highest engine and frame numbers of the batch, quite possibly it is the last Commando to have been made.

33

34

35

36

37. The primary chaincase of the later models has only two inspection caps, the primary chain now having an hydraulic tensioner. The starter motor housing can be seen immediately to the rear of the cylinder block.

38. The use of a left-hand gearchange necessitated a cross-over arrangement from the separate AMC gearbox.

39. A modified left-hand footrest hanger is used on the late models as there is no longer need to incorporate a pivot for the rear brake pedal.

40. The rear brake pedal pivots from the top of the modified right-hand footrest hanger. It has a short, direct linkage to the hydraulic rear brake master cylinder-cum-reservoir.

41. The front disc brake of the later models is mounted on the left-hand side of the wheel and has its caliper in front of, and not behind, the fork leg.

42. To obviate the need for shimming up, the Isolastic mountings were made adjustable on the later models.

37

38

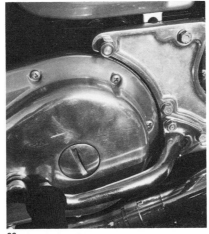
39

41

40

42

43. The timing cover now has an inspection cap to facilitate checking the tension of the timing chain – previously a time-consuming task. Note the tachometer drive take-off from the back of the timing chest.

44. The warning lamps are contained within a small panel between the speedometer and tachometer on the Electric Start models. The ignition switch is now in the centre of this panel.

43

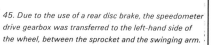

45. Due to the use of a rear disc brake, the speedometer drive gearbox was transferred to the left-hand side of the wheel, between the sprocket and the swinging arm.

44

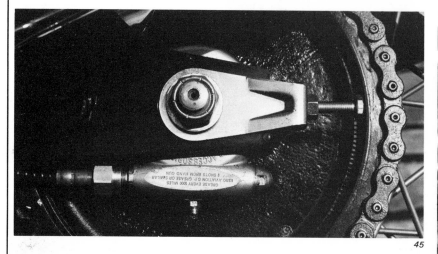

45

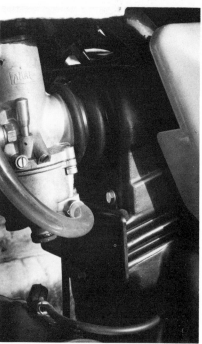

46. The air cleaner box has been changed in design but still utilises rubber bellows for the connections with the carburetter intakes.

46

47. Silencers of the absorption type give a muted exhaust note without a loss in performance.

48. The later type of dualseat provides better rider/passenger comfort and blends in particularly well with the large capacity Interstate petrol tank. The seat hinges sideways.

47

48

49

49. The legend on the left-hand side panel of the Electric Start models.

50. The red and black lining of the petrol tank, against the silver background colour is similar to that used on Nortons in the Bracebridge Street days.

50

51. A selection of Interpol police models awaiting despatch from Andover. Note the single seat and the platform above the rear mudguard on which the two-way radio equipment will be mounted. (Mike Jackson).

52. The late Eric Oliver hurls his Dominator twin/Watsonian Monaco sidecar outfit into a left-hander, with Pat Wise able to do little to keep the sidecar wheel down. He finished 10th in this 1958 Sidecar TT, to win a Bronze Replica, despite the maximum speed of the outfit being at least 40mph down on that of the race leaders. This feat illustrated the stamina of the machine from which the Commando was developed.

53. This shot, taken in the Isle of Man, shows Mick Grant aboard one of the John Player-sponsored works Nortons during the 1973 F750 race. He finished 2nd to his team mate Peter Williams after a brilliant ride on his fly-spattered machine, to ensure Nortons took the first two places. (Mike Jackson).

51

52

53

54. Phil Read accepts the Guild of Motoring Writers Award for the Rider of the Year from Dennis Poore. The year is 1973, when Read was a member of the Norton team. (Mike Jackson).

54

55. For a time, NVT gave support to Belgian Robert Grogg, who won the 1974 European Sidecar Championship on a Wasp sidecar outfit powered by a Commando engine. Here his Manager, Lee Van Dam collects a £500 cheque from Dennis Poore, as Grogg himself was already on his way to the USA. Robbie Rhind Tutt, the builder of the highly successful Wasp motocross outfits, is on the left. (Mike Jackson).

56. This unusual 750cc Commando outfit was specially-made for fire fighting use during race meetings on the Silverstone race circuit. It possessed a high degree of mobility that made it particularly suitable for this kind of use. (Mike Jackson).

57. One of the most successful privately-owned production racing Commandos is the machine owned by

Fran and Celia Ridewood, of Wells, Somerset. Ridden by Bill Marks, this machine took Bill to many wins and lap records and at one time held the fastest lap for production machines during a Hutchinson 100 meeting run over the Brands Hatch Grand Prix Circuit in the reverse direction. Originally owned by the late Ron Wittich as a 750, the machine was acquired by the Ridewoods and developed through to 828cc capacity before being retired from racing in 1979. (Fran and Celia Ridewood).

58. Peter Williams and Dave Croxford pose on standard 850cc and 750cc road-going models, clad in their John Player leathers. The venue is the Thruxton race circuit, where the Norton racing team were based. (Mike Jackson).

55

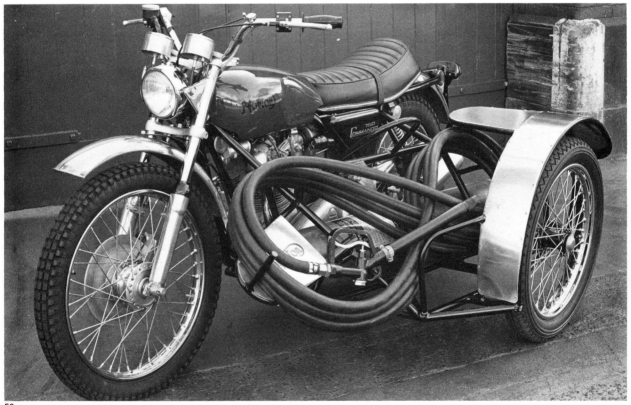

56

57

58

59.

60.

59. *Geoff Duke and his son Peter, the latter of whom worked for Avon Tyres, assisted with tyre testing demonstrations at the time when the new Roadrunner tyres were introduced. (Avon Tyres).*

60. *The double-engined Norton streamliner with which it was hoped to make a World Speed Record bid in the USA. Most of the streamlining has been removed to show the internals, this being the day of the Press launch. (Mike Jackson).*

61. *The late Bob Greene, Editor of* Motorcyclist, *discusses the double-engined Norton with Cook Nielson, then Editor of* Cycle, *during the Press reception. (Mike Jackson).*

62. *The Cosworth twin racing engine that was intended to replace the original Hopwood-designed twin-cylinder Norton engine, had NVT not withdrawn from racing before it was ready for use. (Mike Jackson).*

61.

62.

C1

C2

C1. 750cc Norton Commando models are already
becoming fairly difficult to find, particularly those that
have been well looked after and kept to near original
specification. This 750cc model is owned by Mike
Taverner, of Chippenham, Wiltshire, a member of the
Norton Owners Club.

C2. The left-hand side of Mike Taverner's machine, a
750cc Fastback. Even to the uninitiated there can be
little doubt about the country of origin of the
manufacturer!

C3. This close-up shows the clean lines of the engine and its family likeness to the earlier Norton twins of the Hopwood era.

C3

C4. The distinctive 'Norton' logo in gold looks strikingly effective against the plain, dark green background colour of the petrol tank.

C4

C5. The full-width hub has a very effective front brake of the twin leading shoe type, of pleasing appearance too.

C6. The primary chaincase has three inspection caps, for checking the ignition timing by stroboscope, the primary chain tension, and for making coarse clutch adjustment.

C5

C6

C7

C8

C7. This 850cc Roadster, owned by Chris Rogers of Milborne Port, Dorset, is in near original condition and one of the better examples of its kind. The majority of Commando Owners in the Norton Owners Club have the 850cc models.

C8. The right-hand side of Chris Rogers' 850cc Roadster model. The only major change from original specification is in the fitting of individual air cleaners to the carburetter intakes, in order to dispense with the air cleaner box which is difficult to remove and relies on poor quality rubber bellows for its carburetter connections.

C9. All Commando engines are inclined forward in the frame, a feature that distinguishes them from the earlier 'Atlas' engine from which they were developed.

C10. Only the very early Commando engines used a distributor mounted in the position originally occupied by the magneto of the 'Atlas' engine. All the 850cc engines have the contact breaker points within a separate housing that forms part of the timing cover.

C11. The twin exhaust pipes are joined by a short balance pipe shortly after they emerge from the exhaust ports. The finned retaining rings need to be tightened securely, and checked regularly, to prevent them from working loose and damaging the internal thread of the exhaust ports – a common Commando fault.

C9

C10

C11

Super Profile

C12. This Mark 3A Electric Start 850cc model is owned by Guy Shoosmith of St. Mary Bourne, Wiltshire. An Interstate model, as denoted by the large capacity fuel tank, it was one of the last, if not the last, to leave the Wolverhampton factory ...

C13. ...Still unregistered, and with less than 100 recorded miles on the clock, it forms part of the owner's large collection of historic motorcycles and cars.

C12

C13

C14. Reversion to the traditional Norton colours gave the later 850cc models a particularly distinguished look, reminiscent of Nortons of the past. It is a heavy machine to handle, with limited steering lock.

C14

C15. The matching instruments carry the latter-day NVT logo, the original 'green blob' symbol having, by now, been dropped from all but the company notepaper. The warning lamps now have their own central display panel.

C15

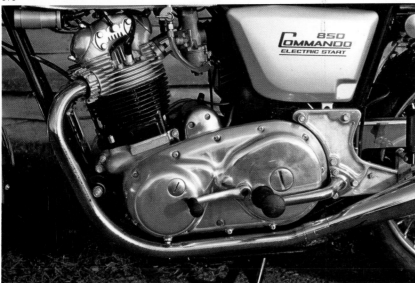

C16. The legend on the side panels tells all, except to say that everything had to be just right for the starter to function as it should. In colloquial terms it was always referred to as the 'electric assister' by those who really knew!

C16

C17. American legislation dictated the transposition of the rear brake and foot gearchange levers to comply with the Japanese practice manufacturers, a sad reflection on the loss of Britain's one-time domination of the world motorcycle market.

C18. This colour photograph illustrates the simple but effective use of the John Player livery at the time of introduction of the 850cc John Player Replica. Sadly, it remained in production for only a little short of a year, in 1974, after which John Player withdrew their sponsorship of the Norton racing team. (Mike Jackson).

C18